Teaching With
Cinderella Stories
From Around the World

by Kathleen M. Hollenbeck

SCHOLASTIC
PROFESSIONAL BOOKS

New York • Toronto • London • Auckland • Sydney
Mexico City • New Delhi • Hong Kong • Buenos Aires

To Alexandra, Kyle, and Kelsie,
for all the Cinderella stories we've shared.

The activities in this book have been reviewed for safety and are meant to be done by children with adult supervision.
The author does not assume any responsibility for injuries or accidents that might result from performing these
activities without proper supervision.

Cover design by Josué Castilleja

Cover and interior illustrations by Delana Bettoli, except page 58 by James Graham Hale

Interior design by Sydney Wright

ISBN: 0-439-18843-1
Copyright © 2003 by Kathleen M. Hollenbeck.
All rights reserved. Printed in the U.S.A.

4 5 6 7 8 9 10   40   09 08 07 06 05 04 03

Contents

Introduction

For centuries, fairy tales have held an important place in the lives of people from one end of the globe to the other. A measure of humanity, a record of tradition, and a gateway for fantasy, the fairy tale has entertained and inspired countless generations. Few tales have been more widely spread than the one known by many as Cinderella. Found in hundreds of variations and set in cultures around the world, Cinderella has been told and retold, preserved and embellished in nearly every language.

Cinderella stories date back as early as 850 A.D., with the first written version of the Chinese tale *Yeh-hsien*. Scholars believe the story existed in multiple cultures even then. Today there are no less than 350 (and perhaps hundreds more) variants of the tale. Differing widely in characters, plot, use of magic, and other details, a common thread binds them all: They each tell the story of a young girl or boy who is mistreated by family or community but is eventually recognized and rewarded for goodness and virtue.

Teaching With Cinderella Stories From Around the World is packed with activities based on ten Cinderella tales from nine nations. Each has its own unique story line and offers insight into its culture, yet the similarities between them make it easy to compare and contrast character, plot, point of view— even footwear—across the stories. Activities, games, and manipulatives extend the tales, sharpen children's cultural awareness, and help them build skills in math, science, language arts, social studies, drama, and music. Read, discuss, dramatize, illustrate, create, compare . . . and enjoy the wonderful, diverse worlds of Cinderella!

How to Use This Book

This book is designed for flexible use; you can share all the Cinderella stories included or choose a few. Select the activities that best meet the needs of your students, and adapt them as you see fit. You can present the stories and activities in any order. For each Cinderella story, you'll find:

❧ a brief introduction to the book.

❧ quick ideas to introduce the story and culture to children.

❧ discussion questions.

❧ skill-building activities arranged by curriculum area (social studies, language arts, math, science, and more).

❧ teacher-tested ideas.

❧ one to three reproducible activity pages.

In addition, you'll find activities that can be used with any Cinderella story (pages 7–15), activities to wrap up your study (pages 77–79), and a list of additional resources (page 80).

To get the most from your Cinderella studies, take time before you begin to do the following:

Set Up a Learning Center

Launch your study by setting up a Cinderella Center in your classroom. Decorate the center with a map of the world. Cut out magazine pictures of people, clothing, homes, and scenery in various countries. Make a cardboard coach that children can actually sit and read in during free time. For a basic coach, use an intact refrigerator box. Lay the box on its side and use a straightedge razor to cut out a door and cut off the top for headroom. Attach circles cut from posterboard to each side. Place two milk crates inside to serve as seats, add throw pillows for royal comfort, and decorate the exterior of the coach with paint or craft paper. **Note:** It need not be in the shape of a pumpkin. Fill the coach with books. (See Additional Resources on page 80.) Stock the center with gift catalogs showing artifacts and objects from different countries, dictionaries with English translations, and laminated samples of international postage stamps. At the entrance to your center, post student-made welcome signs in different languages, such as *Willkommen* (German), *Welkom* (Afrikaans), *Welcome* (English), and *Bienvenidos* (Spanish).

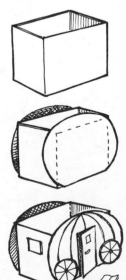

Create Portfolios

Set aside pocket folders in which each child can store charts, mini-books, and other projects related to the Cinderella tales. Encourage children to keep a running glossary of related words and phrases from the stories and cultures. Leave the charts in the learning center so that children can look through their folders and add to them throughout their studies.

Explore Gender Bias and Stereotypes

In many versions of the story, Cinderella is rescued from her plight by magic or through the intervention of a strong male hero. While this is a common theme in fairy tales, it may not reflect modern cultures. For most females today, the ideal is not to be rescued by a prince but to carve one's own success through the use of knowledge, ingenuity, and perseverance. Help children identify the discrepancies that often exist between life in fairy tales and life in reality. Broaden their awareness of gender bias through discussion. Point out stereotypes (of gender, age, class, stepfamilies) whenever they arise. Eventually, children will likely begin pointing them out to you—in these and other stories.

Together, rewrite (or revise aloud) portions of the stories that children wish to change to reflect their own views. Perhaps the prince is the one who needs help, or magic fails and the heroine brings herself to victory. Brainstorm ways Cinderella can establish a fair chore schedule at home, earn spending money on the side, and get to the ball without anyone's help. Give students an active role in shaping fairy tales—and their own views—to reflect self-confidence, ambition, and a creative approach to solving problems.

What Is a Fairy Tale?

Help children understand that a fairy tale is part of a larger group of stories called folktales. Explain that a folktale is a story that was told again and again and was eventually written down. Created to entertain listeners at a time in history when few people could read, folktales were used to explain natural phenomena, explore human relationships and emotions, and teach lessons in moral behavior. The folktales known as fairy tales lend themselves well to fantasy, allowing listeners to escape to a different time and place—a place of enchantment with happy endings and the cottage or castle of one's dreams. Unlike myths and legends, fairy tales are not used to explain natural phenomena or how things came to be. They are simply used to explore human behavior through the gateway of fantasy and to extend the hope that goodness and truth win out in the end.

Activities to Use With Any Cinderella Story

✿ Cinderellas Around the World (Social Studies)

Give each student a copy of the map on page 12 and the glass slippers at right. Have children color the slippers different colors. Then help them locate each of the nine countries featured in these Cinderella stories and glue a slipper to mark the location. You might add to this map each time you read a Cinderella story of a different origin. Have students store their maps in their Cinderella portfolios.

To help students with this activity, display a world map on a bulletin board. As you study each Cinderella story, press a pushpin into the map to show where in the world that story took place. Tie a piece of yarn around the pushpin and extend it to one side of the map. Place a label there and write the title of the story. You might make your labels in the shape of a glass slipper.

✿ Invite Storytellers (Social Studies)

Invite cultural storytellers to visit with your class and share stories, artifacts, and customs from their native lands. These can be professional storytellers or friends and relatives who wish to share their family's heritage.

✿ Hello! Bonjour! (Language Arts)

Use word wheels to introduce basic words from different languages. Cut out two circles with 5-inch diameters (approximately). Use a hole punch to make the center holes. Cut out one-fourth of wheel A. Then place wheel A on top of wheel B and use a brass fastener to join them. When children want to know how to say "hello" in Afrikaans, French, German, or Spanish, they can simply turn the wheel to find out!

To create word wheels for other common words, use a white label to cover the word *hello* on wheel A and write another common word, such as *goodbye* in its place. On wheel B, use white labels to cover the translations for *hello*. Replace these with the translations for the new word. Copy the information on page 8 onto chart paper so that children can cut out and assemble new word wheels.

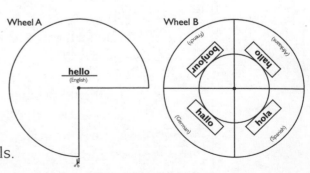

English	Afrikaans	French	German	Spanish
goodbye	tot siens	au revoir	auf wiedersehen	adios
thank you	dankie	merci	danke	gracias
please	asseblief	s´il vous plaît	bitte	por favor
no	nee	non	nein	no
yes	ja	oui	ja	si

❀ Make Character Maps (Language Arts)

Photocopy and distribute the reproducible character map on page 13. Invite children to think about the main character in the story and answer the questions based on that character. Have them write their answers on the character map. Make a new copy for each of the stories. Children can keep the completed reproducibles in their portfolios and use them to compare characters throughout their studies.

Teacher-Tested Idea: Gala Greetings (Language Arts)

After reading a variety of Cinderella stories from around the world, discuss what words might have been spoken when Cinderella first met the prince. What music might have been played as they danced all night long? Provide children with foreign language dictionaries and a variety of cassettes or CDs with music from various countries. With music playing in the background, have children mingle and exchange greetings from many lands.

Contributed by Sue Lorey
Arlington Heights, Illinois

Name _____ Date _____

Compare Cinderella Stories

Title of Story	Main Character	Who Lives With Main Character	Main Character's Wish	Who Helps Main Character Get Wish	How Main Character Gets Wish
Cinderella	Cinderella	stepmother, 2 stepsisters	to go to the ball	fairy godmother	Fairy godmother helps her.
The Irish Cinderlad	Becan	stepmother, father, 3 stepsisters	to have enough to eat	bull	He pulls food from bull's ear.
Princess Furball	Princess Furball	father	to go to the ball	She helps herself.	
Yeh-Shen	Yeh-Shen				
Kongi and Potgi	Kongi				
The Turkey Girl	The Turkey Girl				
The Rough-Face Girl	the Rough-Face Girl				
Cendrillon	Cendrillon				
Mufaro's Beautiful Daughters	Nyasha				
Cinder Edna	Cinder Edna				

Title of Story	Task Main Character Must Do	Animals in the Story	Magic in the Story	Proof of the Main Character's Identity	What Happens to Evil Characters
Cinderella	clean house	mice, rats lizards			
The Irish Cinderlad	defeat bull and dragon	bull and dragon			
Princess Furball	chores	none			
Yeh-Shen	chores	fish			
Kongi and Potgi	chores				
The Turkey Girl	herd turkeys				
Cendrillon	chores				
The Rough-Face Girl	tend the fire				
Mufaro's Beautiful Daughters	tend crops				
Cinder Edna	housework				

❀ Compare Cinderella Stories (Language Arts)

Use the two-page reproducible chart on pages 14–15 to help children compare all ten Cinderella stories in this resource book. Photocopy both pages (you may want to enlarge them) and tape together horizontally. Have children fold the chart in half and store it in their portfolios. After reading and discussing each story, help children fill in the information on the chart and note similarities and differences among the stories they've read so far.

 Teacher-Tested Idea: Fairy Tale Classified   (Language Arts)

Wanted: Students to write wildly imaginative want ads for services or goods needed by their favorite characters in a Cinderella tale. Start this activity by bringing in sample want ads. Discuss the different types of ads and what makes them effective. Then have students choose a character from any of the Cinderella tales they've read and write an imaginary want ad for that character. For example, does the Turkey Girl need help finding the missing turkeys? Will the prince hold a contest to see who can come up with the most recipes for tuna casserole? Might Princess Furball want someone to sew a mattress from her fur coat when she no longer needs it?

Adapted from an idea contributed by VaReane Gray Heese
Springfield Elementary
Springfield, Nebraska

This activity appeared in *Instructor* magazine.

Storyboard (Language Arts)

Explore story elements on a bulletin board modeled after Cinderella's carriage. Use craft paper to create a large pumpkin coach and five white mice. Place the coach on the left side of the bulletin board, and extend five long strips of yarn from it. At the end of each, staple one white mouse. Label the pumpkin with the title of the story. Label each mouse with one of the following questions: "Where does the story take place? Who is the main character? Who are the villains? What does the main character want? How does the character get what she or he wants?" Answer the questions as a class, and write the answers on the mice. As you study each new Cinderella tale, replace the mice with new ones and answer the questions again.

Character Acronyms (Language Arts)

Help children make acronyms for characters in the story. For *The Irish Cinderlad*, an acronym for the main character might be:

Big Feet   Even-tempered   Courageous   Able   Nice

Question of the Week (Language Arts)

Place question strips in a plastic pumpkin. Encourage students to pick one a week and answer the question from a character's point of view. Include questions such as "Prince, how did you feel when Cinderella ran off so suddenly?" and "Cinderella, what was the best part of your big night out?"

 Teacher-Tested Idea: Guess Who? (Language Arts)

Challenge the class to a round of Guess Who? Choose six children to stand in front of the class. Ask each of the six to hold a tagboard strip labeled with the name of a character from any of the Cinderella tales you have studied, such as Yeh-Shen, Cinderella, and Becan. Select one of the children without telling whom you chose. The object is not for the class to guess whom you've chosen but to use the process of elimination to arrive at the answer. One at a time, give clues to help them narrow their choices, such as: "The person I am thinking of had a magic friend." After each clue, children raise their hands and use the information to decide which one should be eliminated from the group. Once a child has been identified, he or she is asked to sit down. When one person is left standing, students will know who was selected.

Adapted from an idea submitted by Marianne Chang

Schilling Elementary

Newark, California

This activity appeared in *Instructor* magazine.

 Pocket Chart
(Language Arts)

On strips of tagboard, write eight sentences that capture the main events in a specific Cinderella tale. Place these in random order in a pocket chart. Invite children to rearrange them to put the events in order as they took place in the story.

Kongi and Potgi
Kongi's father tells her he is going to marry Doki.
Doki and Potgi make Kongi do all of their chores.
An ox helps Kongi clear a rocky field.
A toad helps Kongi fill a water jar.
A hundred sparrows fill the jar of rice.
Angels dress Kongi in fine clothes and take her to the party.
Kongi runs away from the prince.
Kongi marries the prince and forgives Doki and Potgi.

What Time Is It? (Math)

Explore the concept of time as it's presented in Cinderella stories. Have children review the stories to find out and compare when the main character in each Cinderella story had to be home from the big event: before midnight, before sunset, in a half-hour, and so on. Compare the ways in which time is tracked: by clocks and watches, sunlight or dark, and the start or completion of certain events. Talk about time limits children observe in their own lives, such as getting to the bus stop at a specific time and going to bed at a certain hour.

🌹 When the Clock Strikes Twelve (Math)

In several versions of Cinderella, she runs from the ball by the stroke of midnight. Have children explore time concepts by making and using their own interactive clocks. To make the clocks, give each child a small, dessert-sized paper plate, a brass fastener, and two strips of tagboard (2-inches long and 4-inches long) for the clock hands. Using an actual clock as a model, have children write the numerals clockwise on their plates. Then help them use the brass fasteners to attach the hands to the clock face. Together, set the clocks to a specific time, such as ten o'clock. Then ask children, "How many hours will it be until midnight?" and have them calculate the time difference. Continue this activity, providing different times and asking children to calculate the hours left until Cinderella needs to leave the ball.

🌹 What Would They Say? (Drama)

Divide the class into groups of three or four. Let each group choose similar characters from the stories and act out a conversation they might have. What would the stepsisters in *Cinderella* say to the sisters in *The Rough-Face Girl*? What would Cinderella say to Yeh-Shen and Becan? What advice might they give? What compliments might they pay to one another?

🌹 Where Are They Now? (Drama)

Project your students into the future—fairy tale style! Invite them to portray various characters from the fairy tales, and have classmates interview them ten or twenty years after they appeared in the story. How is Cinderella doing as a royal wife? What does Becan do for excitement now that he's had the ultimate adventure and conquered the dragon?

🌹 Sing a Song (Music)

Bring in CDs, cassettes, or sheet music of songs from other cultures. Play the music during free time, or teach children simple songs such as "Frere Jacques."

🌹 Sounds Around the World (Music)

Expose children to instruments that are popular in various cultures, such as the recorder (England), violin (Japan), drum (Africa), and flute (North America). If possible, invite musicians to bring in the instruments and play for the class.

Name _____

Date _____

Cinderellas Around the World

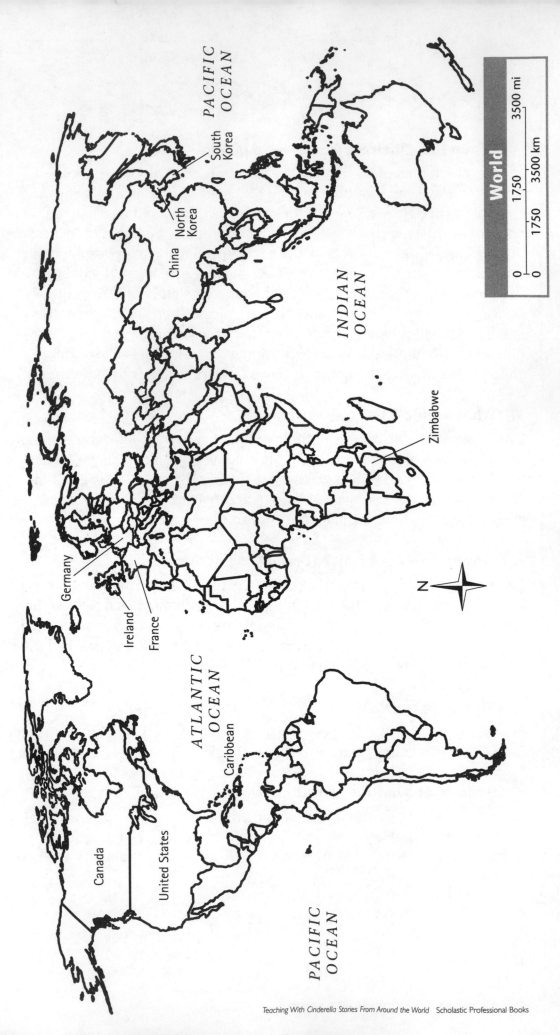

ARCTIC OCEAN

PACIFIC OCEAN

South Korea

North Korea

China

INDIAN OCEAN

Zimbabwe

World

0   1750   3500 km

0   1750   3500 mi

Germany

Ireland

France

ATLANTIC OCEAN

Caribbean

Canada

United States

PACIFIC OCEAN

N

Teaching With Cinderella Stories From Around the World   Scholastic Professional Books

Name _____

Date _____

Make a Character Map

Write three words to describe the character.

How does the character treat others?

What does the character want most?

What makes the character sad?

What is the character's name?

Is the character a girl or a boy?

Where does the character live?

What makes the character happy?

Compare Cinderella Stories

Title of Story	Who Lives With Main Character	Main Character's Wish	Who Helps Main Character Get Wish	How Main Character Gets Wish
Cinderella				
The Irish Cinderlad				
Princess Furball				
Yeh-Shen				
Kongi and Potgi				
The Turkey Girl				
The Rough-Face Girl				
Cendrillon				
Mufaro's Beautiful Daughters				
Cinder Edna				

Title of Story	Task Main Character Must Do	Animals in the Story	Magic in the Story	Proof of the Main Character's Identity	What Happens to Evil Characters
Cinderella					
The Irish Cinderlad					
Princess Furball					
Yeh-Shen					
Kongi and Potgi					
The Turkey Girl					
The Rough-Face Girl					
Cendrillon					
Mufaro's Beautiful Daughters					
Cinder Edna					

FRANCE

Cinderella

BY CHARLES PERRAULT
TRANSLATED BY ANTHEA BELL
(North-South Books, 1999)

In 1697 the French author Charles Perrault published a collection of fairy tales that included the story of Cinderella, or "The Little Glass Slipper." This tale is considered by many to be the traditional Cinderella. In the story, a young girl is forced to be a servant for her stepfamily and she dreams of going to a palace ball. With the help of her fairy godmother, she attends two balls and captures the heart of a prince. The splendor of the palace and the authority given the prince emphasize the importance of royalty in seventeenth-century France, the setting of this story.

Before Reading

Help students find France on a world map or globe. Explain that the story they are about to read was written in France more than 300 years ago and takes place there. Discuss life in France at that time and the importance of royalty. To give children an idea of the splendor of royal life during that time, show them photographs of Versailles, the home of Louis XIV, or visit the official Web site at **www.chateauversailles.fr**. To give children a flavor of life in France today, bring in magazine photographs of famous French landmarks such as the Eiffel Tower, the Seine River, and a typical outdoor café. You might

even serve croissants for a French treat! (Be sure to ask families about food allergies and restrictions first.)

After Reading

After reading the story, ask:

❀ How does Cinderella feel when her stepsisters leave for the ball? Why does she feel that way?

❀ In what way does Cinderella's godmother help her?

❀ What clue does the prince use to find Cinderella?

❀ How do Cinderella's stepsisters feel when they see that the slipper fits her foot? How do you know this?

❀ What kind of person is Cinderella? What parts of the story show this?

Merci! Thank You! *Activity Page* (Social Studies)

No doubt Cinderella held a heart full of gratitude for her fairy godmother, the one responsible for getting her to the ball. How might Cinderella have shown her gratitude? Help children brainstorm ways Cinderella could have thanked her, such as inviting her to dinner or asking her to be the maid of honor at the wedding. Then distribute copies of the reproducible on page 21 and let children create their own moving stories to show Cinderella's gratitude in action. Encourage innovation!

Teacher-Tested Idea: Chores, Chores, Chores (Social Studies)

Discuss with children why it is important to help keep one's home clean. Then talk about why it was unfair that Cinderella was expected to do all the chores in her stepmother's home. At the top of a sheet of notebook paper, have children write, "At home, I am responsible for . . ." Have children prepare a list of their own chores. Record their responses on the chalkboard. Many children may discover that they have similar chores. Use this information to help children create chore graphs. Which chore is most common? Which is the most unique? How many children are responsible for doing one chore? How many have three or more chores?

Contributed by Sue Lorey
Arlington Heights, Illinois

Character Emotions (Social Studies)

Imagine the range of emotions Cinderella must have felt on the day and night of the ball. How did she feel as she helped the sisters get ready? When the fairy godmother appeared out of nowhere? When the pumpkin turned into a coach? Imagine her feelings as she stared up at the palace steps for the very first time. Briefly discuss how Cinderella might have felt at different points in the story. Have children show Cinderella's changing feelings on their faces. Then let each child choose a scene from the story and draw it on paper, centered around an orange juice lid glued into place. Using yarn, movable eyes or buttons, and other craft materials, have children transform their lids into Cinderella's head and face, complete with expression, to show how she felt at that point in the story. (If orange juice lids are unavailable, cut out a paper circle or draw one instead.)

EXTEND IT!

Write a "Dear Diary" heading on the chalkboard. Invite each child to write or dictate a diary entry showing how Cinderella felt at one point in the story. Then have them add an illustration.

Cinder . . . Fella? (Language Arts)

Rewrite the story with a male character in Cinderella's role. Would he have done the same chores back then? How about today? How would he have felt about his chores? What would he have wished for? Who would have come to his aid? After children have shared their stories, read *Prince Cinders*, Babette Cole's entertaining spoof on Cinderella (Putnam, 1997). Set in the 1990s and filled with humorous twists and fun illustrations, this delightful book presents a male perspective on the traditional Cinderella story.

What If? (Language Arts)

Divide the class into groups of four or five students. Ask each group a question that prompts them to think about ways the story of Cinderella would be different if its circumstances changed. Ask questions, such as "What if there had been no fairy godmother? What if the clock stopped working at 11:45 P.M.?" Have each group think about how the new circumstances might affect the story's plot or outcome. Then have them write or act out a new scene.

Make Story Chains (Language Arts)

Give each child three 3- by 5-inch index cards and an 18-inch piece of yarn. Have children illustrate the three index cards to show what happened first in the story, what happened next, and what happened last. Punch a hole in each index card and string them in order on the piece of yarn.

Teacher-Tested Idea: If the Shoe Fits . . . (Language Arts)

What would have happened if one of the stepsisters had the same shoe size as Cinderella? The glass slipper would have fit her, too. Then what might have happened? Have students either write a new ending or debate what would have happened. You might want to take the case to trial, selecting students to pose as Cinderella, the stepsisters, the prince, and a host of witnesses, each telling or writing his or her recollection of what happened on the night of the ball and presenting it before a jury of peers. Whose slipper is it? You be the judge!

Contributed by Sue Lorey
Arlington Heights, Illinois

Match the Beaded Slippers (Math)

Trace children's feet onto tagboard so that each child has one pair of footprints. Have them color the footprints to resemble matching slippers. Give children each a handful of 10–15 beads. Have them glue the beads on both slippers so the two are identical. Collect the slippers, mix them up, and place them in a learning center for children to match during free time.

EXTEND IT!

Have kids make a large bar graph on a bulletin board to show how many kids have each shoe size. Label each column with a shoe size. Label each row with a number. Have each child draw an X in a box to show his or her shoe size. As an alternative, they could glue their slippers on the chart. Then ask children questions about the information, such as "How many people wear a size 3? How many more people wear a size 2?"

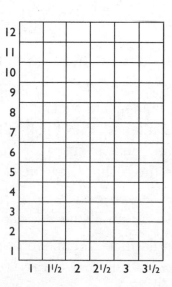

Head to the Ball! *Activity Page* (Math)

How many pumpkins would it take to transport your class to the ball? Based on Cinderella's needs for one person, how many pumpkins, mice, rats, lizards, and glass slippers would the class need? Distribute photocopies of page 22 and review the directions. Help students use simple multiplication to answer each question—for example, if there were 20 students, they would need 40 glass slippers (2 x 20 = 40). You might have children use manipulatives to help them find the answers.

Notice the Artist's Touch (Art)

Invite children to study Loek Koopmans's illustrations and their dreamy, magical quality. Ask children to consider what techniques the artist used to achieve that effect. For example, the use of white and yellow creates a glowing effect; shading makes a dreamy, surreal atmosphere; and the presence of pastel colors, long flowing scarves, and flowers in the air creates a magical aura. Encourage children to experiment with these techniques using watercolor paints.

Pumpkin? Perfect! (Science)

Cinderella's godmother turned a pumpkin into a coach. Why not a different vegetable, such as an acorn squash? Use this simple science study to help students observe the differences between an acorn squash and a pumpkin. Divide the class into groups of four to six students. Give each group one small pumpkin and one acorn squash. Ask them to describe in writing:

❀ the shape, color, and texture of their group's pumpkin and acorn squash.

❀ the weight of the pumpkin and the acorn squash.

❀ the circumference of the pumpkin and the acorn squash. Use lengths of string to measure circumference. Invite students to estimate first by cutting a length they think will wrap around once. Have them use a separate piece of string for an actual measure. Hang estimate strings beside those that show the actual circumference.

❀ the inside appearance of the pumpkin and the acorn squash. (Use a sharp knife to cut pumpkins and acorn squash for your students.)

❀ the similarities and differences between a pumpkin and an acorn squash.

Adapted from the activity "Seasonal Fruit Fun," published in A *Year of Hands-On Science* by Lynne Kepler (Scholastic, 1996).

Merci! Thank You!

Thanks to her fairy godmother, Cinderella's life changed forever. Draw pictures on the story strip below. Show how Cinderella might have thanked her fairy godmother for all she did. Then cut out the story strip. Slide it into the story mover. Pull the story strip and show Cinderella's thanks in action!

Cut on dotted lines only.

Story Mover

Story Strip

4

3

2

1

Head to the Ball!

How many pumpkins would it take to bring your whole class to Cinderella's ball?

Look at the supplies Cinderella needed for one person. How many students are in your class? Figure out how many of each your class would need.

 If Cinderella needed ___**1**___ pumpkin,

our class would need _____ pumpkins.

If Cinderella needed ___**6**___ mice,

our class would need _____ mice.

 If Cinderella needed ___**2**___ rats,

our class would need _____ rats.

If Cinderella needed ___**5**___ lizards,

our class would need _____ lizards.

The Irish Cinderlad

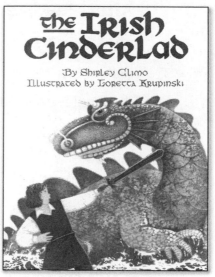

BY SHIRLEY CLIMO
(HarperCollins, 1996)

Based on an Irish folktale, *The Irish Cinderlad* is one of the few Cinderella stories in existence with a male main character. Translated from the Irish language in the nineteenth century, the story tells of a young boy with unusually large feet who is cast out by his stepfamily and left to fend for himself. He befriends a dangerous bull and as a result receives the power to defeat enemies and save the life of a princess. *The Irish Cinderlad* offers a rich taste of Irish culture—from the scenic green fields and thatched-roof cottages to boiled turnips and partridge pie. It also contains the element of exaggeration so often cherished in Irish folklore.

Before Reading

Before reading the story, help students locate Ireland on a world map or globe. Tell them that Ireland is often called the Emerald Isle for its vast green fields. Explain that the country is entirely surrounded by water, which makes it an island. Show students photographs of towns, cities, castles, and countryside scenes in Ireland. To give children a flavor of Irish culture, play recordings of Irish music and read aloud limericks (see Mimic a Limerick on page 26). You might also share fun facts, such as the tradition of the Blarney Stone. This rock is world famous because legend has it that whoever kisses the stone will receive the gift of eloquence. The Blarney Stone is embedded in the walls of Blarney Castle, which was built in 1444.

RELATED RESOURCES

Teachnet.com provides lessons plans about St. Patrick's Day.
http://www.teachnet.com /lesson/seasonal/stpats 031099.html

Ireland (True Books) by Brendan January (Children's Press, 1999) describes Irish history and geography for children ages 9–12. Includes photographs.

After Reading

After reading the story, ask:

❋ How does Becan let the bull know that he wants to be friends?

❋ Why does the Bull tell Becan to twist off his tail?

❋ In what ways does the bull's tail help Becan?

❋ How does Princess Finola feel about Becan? Why does she feel that way? What parts of the story show you this?

❋ How long does it take Princess Finola to find Becan? Why does it take so long to find him?

Want Ads (Social Studies)

Becan was sent to be a cowherd. What other kinds of jobs would be suitable for a person with big and powerful feet? Help children think of jobs—fun and serious—that Becan would be qualified for by virtue of his shoe size. Let children work alone or in small groups to write and illustrate an advertisement for such a job.

Cultivate Kindness (Social Studies)

Rather than being cruel to the bull, Becan treated him kindly—discovering friendship instead of fear. Help children explore this citizenship connection and recognize that treating others with kindness can result in friendship rather than animosity. Select several volunteers to act as Becan and the bull, dramatizing three separate scenes: Becan befriending the bull, Becan running from the bull, and Becan challenging the bull. What might have happened in each instance? Which choice was best for Becan and the bull? Why?

If Boots Could Talk (Language Arts)

Becan walked many miles in his big black boots. How would his boots have described him if they had been able to talk? Cut out an enormous black boot from heavy construction paper or posterboard. Hang it on an easel or chart. Provide white chalk or pastel gel pens and call on volunteers to write words on the boot that describe Becan's character: *brave, honest, kind,* and so on.

An Irish Touch (Language Arts)

Sample the flavor of the Irish language with this pocket chart activity. Write each of the words below from the story on a sentence strip cut to size. The left column shows words from the story; the right column shows their English translations.

Place the Irish words in a column along the left side of a pocket chart. Then place the English translations on the right side of the chart, in random order. After reading the story together, invite children to come up to the chart and match each Irish word to its English translation.

Becan	Little One
wee	tiny
lad	boy
hie	hurry
arhach	giant
slan	good-bye
'tis	it is

Truly Tall Tales (Language Arts)

In *The Irish Cinderlad*, young Becan's feet were "so large he'd splash a puddle dry just by stepping in it." Such exaggeration is found in a family of folklore called tall tales. Tall tales were created to entertain others by stretching the truth and making characters and circumstances larger than life. Help children find other examples of tall-tale exaggeration in this story and others. Then have them write and illustrate their own exaggerated sentences or stories about something they have done or experienced.

Roll a Story *Activity Page* (Language Arts)

Together, determine six significant events that took place in *The Irish Cinderlad*. Write these on the board and number them in order. Distribute copies of the reproducible on page 28. On the corresponding square of the story cube, have children draw a picture to represent each event. Then have them cut along the dotted lines, fold as indicated on the solid lines, and tape together to make a cube. Invite children to use the cube to:

❀ retell the story aloud, turning the cube as they narrate it.

❀ act out portions of the story. Roll the cube and act out the scene that lands on top.

❀ change the story. Roll the cube and revise the scene that lands on top.

❀ make a diorama of whichever scene lands on top.

Mimic a Limerick (Language Arts)

Expose children to a fun kind of poetry that shares the name of a county in Ireland, the limerick. Read aloud limericks from Jack Prelutsky's *For Laughing Out Louder: More Poems to Tickle Your Funnybone* (Knopf, 1995). After children understand the tempo of the humorous verse, ask them to mimic a limerick and write one about Becan or something make-believe, such as a dragon.

Becan's Big Boots (Math)

How big were Becan's boots? Try this fun estimation activity for an inside look at volume. Bring in a large men's work boot. Ask students to estimate how many golf balls (empty film canisters, beanbags, foam packing chips, or other items) it would take to fill the boot. Collect all estimates. Then, fill the boot to capacity, ten items at a time.

Tasty Math (Math)

With help from you and adult volunteers, have children measure and mix the ingredients to make Irish soda bread, based on the recipe below.

⊠ Irish Soda Bread ⊠

4 cups flour
3/4 cup butter or margarine
1 cup sugar
4 teaspoons baking powder
1/2 teaspoon salt
1 cup raisins

1 tablespoon caraway seeds
1 egg
1 cup milk
2 teaspoons cinnamon mixed with
2 tablespoons granulated sugar

Directions

1. Blend flour and butter or margarine until there are no lumps in the batter.
2. Measure and add the next five ingredients.
3. Mix thoroughly.
4. Beat egg and milk together, and add this to the dry ingredients.
5. Press into greased 9-inch square pan.
6. Knead dough gently with floured knuckles.
7. Sprinkle dough with mix of cinnamon and sugar.
8. Bake 50 minutes in an oven heated to 375° F.

Make a Talking Bull (Art)

Use construction paper to make a bull that talks! Here's how:

1. Hold an 8½- by 11-inch sheet of construction paper vertically.

2. Fold the paper in half from top to bottom.

3. Do the same with an 8½- by 5-inch sheet of white paper.

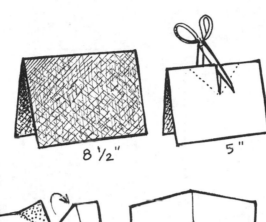

8 ½"   5 "

4. Hold the white paper by the fold. Cut a 2-inch line in the center of the fold.

5. Fold back the edges where you have cut to make two triangular flaps.

6. Open the paper and press the flaps through the opening. Press creases firmly to form the shape of an animal's mouth or beak.

7. Mount the white paper on the construction paper by gluing the outside edges.

8. Draw eyes and other features to turn the character into a bull.

9. Manipulate the paper until the bull "talks."

Using the bull as a puppet, have students take on the point of view of the bull in the story. How did he feel about Becan? What was his life like before he met Becan? You might also want to have students pair up with partners and take turns being the bull and a reporter who interviews him for a local newspaper.

Roll a Story

Think of six important events from the story.

Draw a picture of each event in order from 1 to 6.

Cut along the dotted lines.

Fold along the solid lines.

Tape together to form a cube.

1

2

5   **3**   **6**

4

GERMANY

Princess Furball

BY CHARLOTTE HUCK
(Greenwillow Books, 1989)

PRINCESS FURBALL

CHARLOTTE HUCK · ANITA LOBEL

Princess Furball resembles Jacob and Wilhelm Grimm's tale of Allerleirauh, or The Many Furred Creature. In this and similar tales, the heroine is about to be forced into marriage and escapes. She conceals her identity until her cleverness attracts the attention and affection of a kind and noble king. This story shows a glimpse of life long ago in a castle in Germany. The setting and climate play a major role in the story: The princess escapes deep into a forest in the middle of winter. She wears a coat made from the fur of a thousand different animals, a bridal gift from her father.

Before Reading

Explain that this story takes place long ago in two different castles in Germany. Talk with students about castles as a common setting for fairy tales, and explain that they can still be found in countries such as Germany. Point out Germany on a world map or globe. To help students visualize the story, show photographs of castles and forests in Germany, such as the Black Forest, the Bavarian Forest, and the Bohemian Forest. If you have Internet access, take your students for an online tour of five German castles at **http://www.mediaspec.com/castles/index.html**. This site features photographs of five majestic castles in Germany as well as sketches of their interior layouts.

RELATED RESOURCES

Visit Think Quest's Cultural Connections and click on Germany for maps, photos, and other information.
http://library.thinkquest .org/50055/index.shtml

After Reading

After reading the story, ask:

❀ Why does the princess leave home?

❀ What items does the princess tell her father she must have before she would wed the ogre? Why does she choose those gifts?

❀ How does the princess end up at the king's castle?

❀ Why does she drop the ring, the thimble, and the spinning wheel into the king's soup?

❀ How does the king know that Furball was the princess he had danced with at the ball?

Coat of Kindness (Social Studies)

Create a class coat of one hundred furs—decorated with kindness! Cut or tear at least one hundred small patches of brown, tan, black, and gray construction paper to resemble Princess Furball's coat of a thousand furs. Sketch an outline of the coat on a bulletin board. Each time you or someone in your class sees a child performing an act of kindness, write the act on a fur patch and let the child who acted kindly glue the patch on the coat. When the coat is complete, reward the whole class with a movie during recess, extra gym time, or another favored treat.

Goods or Services? (Social Studies)

What do candy bars, eggs, and bicycles have in common? They are goods— items people buy and sell. Haircuts, dental cleanings, and manicures are services. Explain that Princess Furball went from having goods and services provided for her as a princess to performing services for the king when she cooked and cleaned as a servant in his home. Then further reinforce the difference between goods and services with this simple activity. On separate index cards, write a variety of goods and services people might find in their community today. (See sample list on page 31.) Divide the class into groups, and give each group a handful of cards. Have group members work together to divide the cards into two piles: one for goods and one for services. Go around the room and ask each group to read aloud their goods pile and then their services pile, making corrections as needed. Then ask each group to look at their cards again. Have them

write two places they might go to purchase each good or find each service. The places can be generic, such as the supermarket, or specific locations in the community, such as Joe's Burger Hut.

EXTEND IT!

Place the index cards near a pocket chart that has two headings: "Goods" and "Services." During free time, children can read the cards, determine whether they describe goods or services, and place them in the pockets under the appropriate side heading.

Goods: toothbrush, shampoo, doughnut, furniture, pizza, hammer, coat, boots, notebook, vacuum cleaner, computer, radio

Services: haircut, dental cleaning, garbage pickup, snowplowing, lawn mowing, firefighting, teaching, banking, newspaper delivery, mail delivery, bus driving

Who's Under the Coat? *Activity Page* (Language Arts)

What kind of person hid under the coat of a thousand furs? Help children examine the princess's character—and make shape books at the same time. Distribute copies of the reproducible on page 33. In the boxes, have children complete the character web by writing six traits that describe Princess Furball, such as quiet, hardworking, and clever. Then ask children to cut out the coat and fold on the lines so that it covers the character web. They can then use crayons to decorate the outside of the coat with colorful patches.

Make a Story Quilt (Language Arts)

Divide the class into pairs and give each pair a different-colored paper square. Assign each pair a different event from *Princess Furball* and have them illustrate the scene and write one sentence to describe it. Work together to put the finished pictures in order and staple them on a bulletin board in rows to make a story quilt that retells the tale of Princess Furball.

Star in Your Own Fairy Tale (Language Arts)

Princess Furball didn't need a fairy godmother to change her life. Her own ingenuity saved her from a bad marriage and attracted the attention of a king. Talk briefly with children about the ways Princess Furball used her strengths and talents to look after herself and carve her own success. Invite

children to tell what they consider to be their strengths and talents. Are they kind to others? Good at math? Invite children to focus on one of their strengths and write about it in a short fairy tale.

Retell by Rebus (Language Arts)

With children's help, brainstorm eight sentences that tell the story of Princess Furball. Write these on sentence strips. On smaller strips, have children draw pictures to represent common or significant words in the sentences, such as *coat*, *walnut*, and *king*. Then invite children to place the sentence strips in the chart and take turns retelling the story aloud, inserting pictures over words to make a rebus.

Fractions of Fur *Activity Page* (Math)

Reinforce fractions with this problem-solving activity. Distribute copies of the reproducible on page 34, and review the directions with students. Explain that the coat has 40 patches and that children will follow the directions to color some of the patches. Discuss the concept that they will color a fraction of the patches one color, a fraction of the patches another color, and so on. Depending on your students' grasp of fractions, you may wish to have them complete the page independently or as a group. When students have finished coloring, ask them what fraction of the patches are red, blue, and so on.

Crunch Bunch (Art)

Who says the gingerbread man is the only cookie with character? Prepare cookies ahead of time by rolling out refrigerated sugar cookie dough and cutting it with a cookie cutter in the shape of a gingerbread man. Bake one cookie for each child in your class, and a few extras in case any break. Provide tubes of frosting and bowls of decorations such as sprinkles, raisins, candy-covered chocolates, red hots, and licorice strands. Have children wash their hands with antibacterial soap. Then invite them to decorate the cookies to represent characters in *Princess Furball*.

Name _____

Date _____

Who's Under the Coat?

In each box, write a character trait that describes Princess Furball.
Cut out the coat. Then fold on the dotted lines to hide the web.

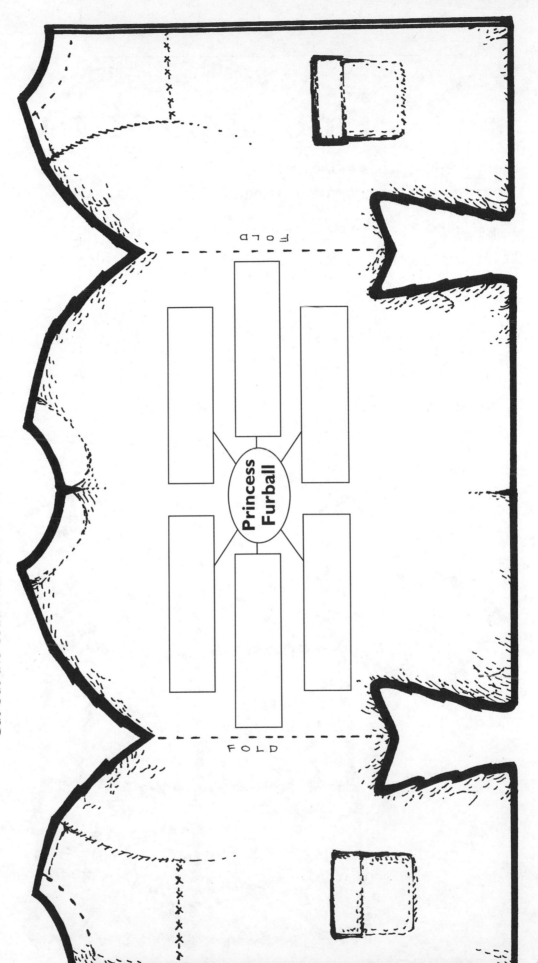

FOLD

FOLD

Princess Furball

Fractions of Fur

There are 40 patches of fur on the coat.
Use crayons to color them according to the directions below.

1 Use a red crayon to color 10 patches.　　**3** Use a yellow crayon to color 5 patches.

2 Use a blue crayon to color 10 patches.　　**4** Use a green crayon to color 15 patches.

What fraction of the patches are red? _____

What fraction of the patches are blue? _____

What fraction of the patches are yellow? _____

What fraction of the patches are green? _____

What fraction of the patches are red or blue? _____

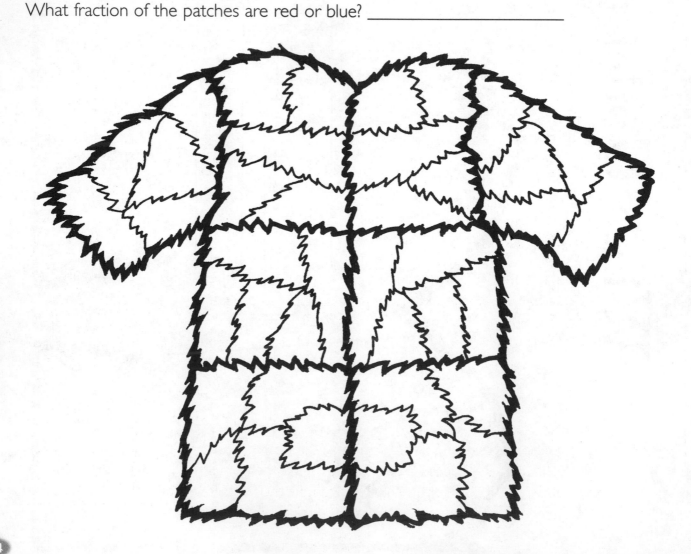

Teaching With Cinderella Stories From Around the World Scholastic Professional Books

Yeh-Shen
A Cinderella Story From China

RETOLD BY AI-LING LOUIE
(Philomel Books, 1982)

The Chinese story of Yeh-Shen (also spelled Yeh-hsien) was written during the T'ang dynasty (618-907 A.D.). It is the earliest recorded Cinderella story in history. In this version of the tale, a young girl is treated harshly by her stepmother and finds solace in the friendship of a fish. When the fish dies, its bones contain a spirit of kindness that transforms the young girl's life. The text and illustrations make this version unique from other Cinderella tales in the way they reflect Chinese culture. Respect for spirits, traditional Chinese dress and manner, and intricate Chinese artistry are inherent in both words and pictures.

Before Reading

Help children find China on a world map or globe. Then tell them that the story they are about to read takes place in China long ago. China, the largest country in East Asia and the fourth largest in the world, has a history that extends back in time more than 4,000 years. The country is separated from its neighbors by natural barriers such as ocean, mountains, and desert. The Great Wall was built in the North, where there are no such barriers. Droughts, floods, and other natural disasters are common in China, a land that encompasses a wide range of climates. As a result, Daoism (or Taoism), an important philosophy of China, stresses the importance of a harmonious relationship between people and nature. Ask children to notice how the characters in *Yeh-Shen* interact with nature and what consequences follow.

After Reading

After reading the story, ask:

❋ Why does Yeh-Shen feel that her only friend is a fish?

❋ What does the stepmother do when she learns that Yeh-Shen has a pet fish?

❋ Why does Yeh-Shen begin talking to the bones of her fish?

❋ In what ways do the fish bones help Yeh-Shen?

❋ Why does Yeh-Shen take the slipper from the pavilion?

Pumpkin Glyphs (Language Arts)

A glyph is a visual organizer—a picture that tells a story. Help children create their own pumpkin-coach glyphs based on *Yeh-Shen*, *Cinderella*, or *The Irish Cinderlad*. Each student needs three 8½- by 11-inch sheets of construction paper (orange, white, and green), one 8½- by 15-inch sheet (any color), pencil, scissors, a glue stick, and a copy of the reproducible on page 39.

1. Have children cut out a pumpkin shape, using the entire sheet of orange paper. They should then glue it onto the large sheet of paper.

2. Review the legend on the reproducible and point out the wheel, window, and stem templates.

3. Explain to children that they will choose one of the Cinderella stories to represent in their glyph.

4. Based on the legend, students should trace, cut out, and glue the templates to create their pumpkin glyph. For the last question, they should draw spokes on each wheel.

EXTEND IT!

Invite children to share completed glyphs with the class. Let classmates try to figure out which story each glyph represents. Then make a graph to show how many glyphs represent *Cinderella*, *The Irish Cinderlad*, and *Yeh-Shen*.

Teacher-Tested Idea: Posing Proverbs (Language Arts)

The proverb "If the shoe fits, wear it" fits in beautifully with the story of Cinderella. Use it as a springboard to a fun—and funny—language

arts lesson. Although adults are familiar with proverbs, young children generally are not. Explain what a proverb is, and provide several examples of these wise old sayings. Then think of other proverbs to use in this activity. Write the first part of a proverb on the chalkboard and ask children to come up with several endings. Children will enjoy coming up with their own endings, such as:

"Children should be seen and not . . . have to go to school."
"It's always darkest before . . . the vampires come out."
"You can lead a horse to water, but you can't . . . take a chicken!"

At the end of the lesson, tell how each proverb really ends. Briefly discuss what it means.

Contributed by Natalie Vaughan
Rancho Encinitas Academy
Encinitas, California

Extra! Extra! (Language Arts)

How might the headlines have read if newspapers long ago had reported on the story of Yeh-Shen? Ask students to pretend they are newspaper journalists reporting on some of the public events in the story. These events should include the arrival of a beautiful, mysterious girl at the feast, the kingdomwide search for the owner of the golden slipper, the king's decision to display the slipper, and Yeh-Shen's transformation from a maiden in rags to the wife of a king. Depending on the age and skill level of your students, have them write headlines and/or brief news articles describing one or more events from a spectator's point of view. Invite your budding journalists to illustrate their work.

Tiny Tangrams Activity Page (Math)

Play an ancient Chinese puzzle game—and exercise math and critical-thinking skills. Have children cut out the seven shapes at the top of the reproducible on page 40. Let them practice combining the shapes in different ways to make objects, animals, and whatever else they wish. Then challenge children to try to re-create the shapes shown at the bottom of the reproducible. Urge children to work in groups to solve the puzzles that require five pieces. Answers may vary. Possible answers are shown at right.

Fish

Slipper

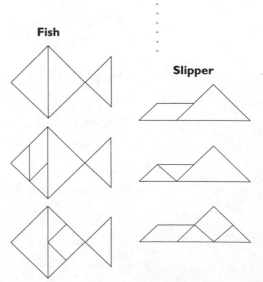

Make a Venn diagram using Hula-Hoops and slippers from home. Have each child bring in a slipper. Overlap two or three Hula-Hoops on the classroom floor to serve as a Venn diagram. In advance, label index cards with qualities a slipper might possess, such as "New," "Fuzzy," "Has a character on it," and "Not mine." Place one label under each Hula-Hoop, and have children put their slippers in whichever hoop applies. Discuss the results, paying special attention to what it means if someone places a slipper outside all the hoops or in the overlapping sections.

Contributed by Natalie Vaughan
Rancho Encinitas Academy
Encinitas, California

Fish Facts (Math)

Yeh-Shen's pet fish was central to her happiness in the story. Draw on the fish theme with this art-related math activity. Cut out fish shapes from kitchen sponges. Have children dip them in paint and press onto paper to make repeating patterns (red fish/blue fish/red fish) or math problems (3 fish + 2 fish = 5 fish).

Bright Backgrounds (Art)

Ask children to look closely at the artwork in *Yeh-Shen*. Nearly every page has patterned fish scales as a backdrop. Provide drawing paper, crayons, and colored chalk or pastels. Have children use chalk and crayons to draw a pattern of fish scales as a border around the page. Then have them use crayons to draw a picture in the center. Encourage them to draw their favorite scene from the story.

EXTEND IT!

Use the same patterning technique to create a story banner. Have children draw fish scales as a border around a long mural. Assign small groups different parts of the story: beginning, middle, and end. Let each group draw pictures on the mural to retell their part of the story, depicting the first part of the story to the far left and the last to the right.

Pumpkin Glyphs

1) Was the main character a boy or a girl?

Wheel Size	Small	Large
	Boy	Girl

2) Does the story include a slipper or a boot?

Windows in Carriage	Two Windows	One Window
	Slipper	Boot

3) Was the main character helped by an animal or a person?

Stem	Pointing Left	Pointing Right
	Animal	Person

4) How many stepsisters did the main character have?

Spokes on Each Wheel	2 Spokes	3 Spokes	4 Spokes	5 Spokes
	2 Stepsisters	3 Stepsisters	4 Stepsisters	5 Stepsisters

Stem Pointing Right

Stem Pointing Left

Large Wheel

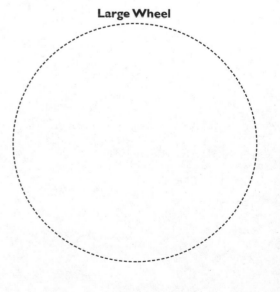

Window

Small Wheel

Teaching With Cinderella Stories From Around the World   Scholastic Professional Books

Tiny Tangrams

Cut out the shapes below.

Try making this fish.
Use 3 shapes.
Use 5 shapes.

Try making this slipper.
Use 2 shapes.
Use 3 shapes.
Use 4 shapes.

Teaching With Cinderella Stories From Around the World   Scholastic Professional Books

Kongi and Potgi: A Cinderella Story from Korea

BY OKI S. HAN

(Dial Books for Young Readers, 1996)*

* New copies of this title may not be available. We recommend borrowing a
copy from your school or local library or purchasing a used copy online.

A tale well-known and loved in Korea, *Kongi and Potgi* tells the story of a young girl who endures hard times and is eventually rewarded for her kindness. The story is filled with intricate details of traditional Korean life, from the importance of rice as a staple and the warmth of thatched homes made of clay to the ancient Korean belief that spirits aid and protect their descendants, appearing in the form of animals.

Before Reading

Before reading the story, help students understand the importance of rice in the Korean diet. Most Koreans eat rice daily, which accounts for the vast expanse of rice fields across the country. Another familiar sight in Korea is outdoor markets, where vendors sell fresh fruits and vegetables. Students will see both of these in *Kongi and Potgi*. Before reading the story, explain that the Korean Peninsula is divided into two countries: North Korea and South Korea. Help students locate both countries on a world map or globe.

After Reading

After reading the story, ask:

❧ How does Kongi feel when her father tells her he plans to remarry? Why does she feel this way?

RELATED RESOURCES

Based on an exhibit at the Seattle Asian Art Museum, *A Visit to Grandfather's House* explores Korean lifestyle through a display of a traditional Korean home in Grandfather's time. Includes lesson plans. **www.seattleartmuseum. org/Exhibit/Archive/ grandfathershouse/ default.htm**

Good-Bye, 832 Shin Dang Dong by Frances Park (National Geographic Society, 2002) tells the story of a young girl moving from Korea to the United States and the cultural differences she experiences.

❧ Why doesn't Kongi's father stop his new wife from treating Kongi harshly?

❧ How do the animals help Kongi? Why do you think they help her?

❧ How does Kongi prove that she owns the slipper?

❧ What kind of person is Kongi? What parts of the story show you this?

A Little Bit Faster Now (Social Studies)

Together, list the various jobs Kongi had to do in the story: washing clothes, sewing by hand, hoeing fields, filling a water jar with water for washing and cooking, drying and removing rice from its shell. Write each task in the left column of a two-column chart. In the right column, ask children to tell how the job has been made easier today by machinery or other modern conveniences, such as plumbing. Then add to the chart, inviting children to think of other jobs that were more difficult long ago than they are today, such as washing dishes and obtaining food.

Job	What Has Made It Easier Today
washing clothes	washing machine
sewing by hand	sewing machine
hoeing fields	tractors and plows
filling water jar	faucets, sinks, tubs
drying and hulling rice	harvesting and hulling machines

What About Rice? (Social Studies)

In this story, Kongi is told to dry and hull the rice. Help children better understand the importance of rice in the Asian diet and the process involved in harvesting, drying, and hulling it. Share the following facts about rice and its production. Write each fact on the board and briefly discuss each one.

Facts About Rice

1. Rice is one of the world's most important crops.

2. More than half the people in the world eat rice daily.

3. Rice grows in climates that are wet and warm.

Following this, divide the class into eight groups, and give each group one sentence strip describing how rice is grown and processed. Have group members work together to illustrate their sentence, using reference materials as needed. Staple the sentence strips to the pictures. Make a flowchart by posting the pictures in order with arrows between them.

How Rice Is Grown and Processed

1. Rice grows in fields covered with water. Water helps the rice grow and keeps pests away.

2. Farmers drain the fields before harvest and then use machines to cut down the plants and divide the grains from the stalks.

3. Wet rice is machine-dried and cleaned. Machines then remove the covering (hull) from each kernel.

4. Rice with only the hull removed is called brown rice. It is the most nutritious kind of rice.

5. When machines remove the hull and layers of bran underneath it, the rice is called white rice.

Who Helped Kongi? *Activity Page* (Language Arts)

Make a lift-the-flap book of riddles that children can solve to recall Kongi's helpers. Distribute copies of the reproducible on page 46. Have children cut along both dotted lines and then cut around the flaps on side A. (You may want to poke a hole in each flap to make it easier for children to cut.) Have children place side A on top of side B so the flaps line up with the pictures. Glue the pages together along the edges only. Let children read the riddles and lift the flaps to see the answers underneath. Encourage them to take the page home to share the riddles—and the story as they remember it—with friends and family members.

How Impossible? *Activity Page* (Language Arts)

Compare the impossible tasks Kongi was given with the impossible tasks Becan faced in *The Irish Cinderlad*. Give each student three copies of the reproducible on page 47. On the first copy of the reproducible, have children answer the questions about Becan's and Kongi's first tasks. (You may want to do this as a large- or small-group activity.) When finished, do the same on the next page for the second tasks. Then have them answer the questions about the third tasks on the last page.

Becan's Tasks	**Kongi's Tasks**
1. befriending the bull	1. hoeing the soil
2. defeating the ogre	2. filling the water jar
3. saving the princess	3. hulling the rice

Slipper Match (Language Arts)

Cut simple glass slippers out of tagboard. Write a compound word on each slipper and then cut the slipper in half to separate the words. During free time, have children match the slippers to create compound words.

Hint: For a math alternative, write math facts on one half of the slipper and the answers on the other. Have children match each equation with the correct answer.

Make Paper Lanterns (Art)

In many countries, people hang colorful lights or lanterns as decorations for festivals and other celebrations. Help your students make paper lanterns to hang in your classroom in honor of the celebration that Kongi had hoped to attend. To make a paper lantern, follow these steps:

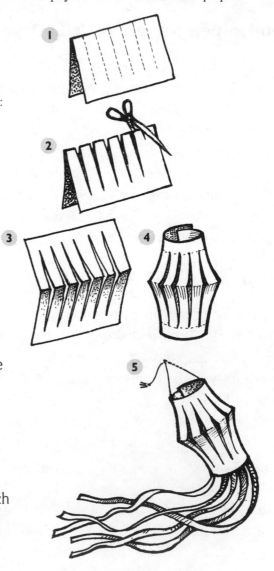

1. Fold a piece of 8$\frac{1}{2}$- by 11-inch construction paper in half horizontally.

2. Cut six 8-inch slits along the fold, leaving 1 inch uncut on either end.

3. Open the paper and lay it vertically on a desk with the fold bending up.

4. Bring together the left and right sides of the paper in the back and staple. This should result in a long, vertical tube with slotted strips that bend outward.

5. Attach string to the top of the lantern for hanging. Attach colorful crepe paper strips to the bottom for decoration.

Fill and Spill (Math)

Fill a dishpan with uncooked rice and place it on a table or counter in your classroom. Place a 4-ounce measuring scoop and a series of plastic containers nearby, such as a small margarine tub, a large margarine tub, a 1- and 2-pound deli container, and a 16-ounce drinking cup.

Invite children to estimate how many scoops it will take to fill the different containers. Leave a log nearby for children to record their predictions and results in chart form.

Container	Estimated Number of Scoops	Actual Number of Scoops
small tub		
large tub		
1-lb container		
2-lb container		
16-oz cup		

Animals of Korea (Science)

In the story, Kongi is helped by an ox, a toad, and one hundred sparrows. Are these animals native to Korea? What other animals might have appeared in the story? Divide the class into groups. Have each group consult reference books, wildlife encyclopedias, or nature magazines to learn which animals live in Korea. Invite each group to choose and draw an animal native to Korea. Then have them write facts they have learned about the animals. Connect the animals and facts to make a mobile or classroom banner for display. Then, based on what they know about their animal, have each group discuss ways they could add on to the story of Kongi and Potgi. How might the animal have appeared in the story? What other tasks might the animal have helped Kongi do?

"My Word!" Said the Bird (Drama)

Have children take on the roles of animals in Kongi and Potgi. Let them take turns telling the story from their points of view, telling how and why they helped Kongi, how Kongi treated them, how the stepmother and stepsister might have treated them, and so on. If you have time, have children make sock puppets or simple masks to represent the characters they portray. (Help children make masks out of felt, paper bags, paper plates, or shoe box lids.)

Who Helped Kongi?

B

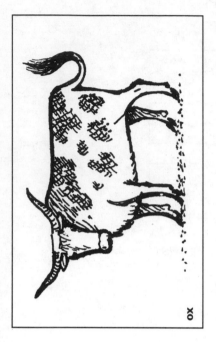

ox

toad

sparrows

A

The soil was hard and rocky.
Kongi's hoe broke in two.
I came along to help her.
I gave her apples, too.
Who am I?

Kongi couldn't fill the jar,
no matter how she tried.
I jumped into the water jar
and plugged the hole inside.
Who am I?

Grains of rice were everywhere—
a task too large for one.
We hulled the rice and filled the jar,
and soon the job was done.

The Turkey Girl: A Zuni Cinderella Story

RETOLD BY PENNY POLLOCK

(Little, Brown and Company, 1996)

The Turkey Girl comes from a nineteenth-century collection of Zuni folktales. In this tale, a young girl herds turkeys for a living. With gratitude for her faithfulness, the turkeys transform her into a vision of beauty so that she can attend a dance. They ask that she return to the turkey cage by sundown. Unlike the fairy tale ending of the traditional Cinderella story, the Zuni version presents the harsh reality of what happens when promises are broken—especially promises made to Mother Earth. As drums beat and braves dance, the story teaches a lesson on loyalty and imparts the beauty and essence of the Zuni culture.

Note: *The Turkey Girl* represents a popular category of folktales often shared in Native American culture: the how-and-why tale. These are also known as *pourquoi* tales. This tale explains why the turkeys live apart from people.

Before Reading

Help students find New Mexico and Arizona on a map. Explain that *The Turkey Girl* takes place long ago and tells about a tribe of Native Americans called the Zuni that lived in northern New Mexico near the Arizona border. (The Zuni still live in this area today.) The Zuni lived by farming the land and growing foods such as corn, beans, and squash. Throughout the year, the Zuni held many religious dances and ceremonies, at which many tribes danced long into the night. One of these dances is described in *The Turkey Girl*.

How Impossible?

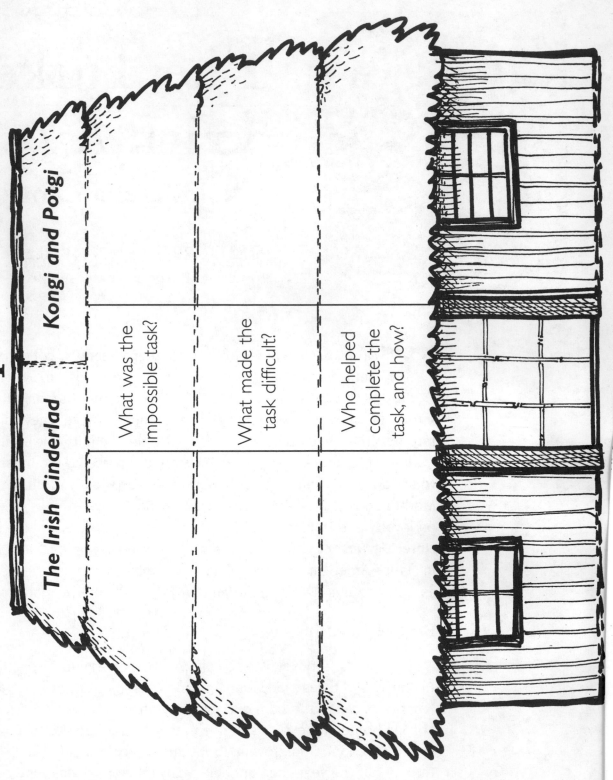

The Irish Cinderlad	Kongi and Potgi
What was the impossible task?	
What made the task difficult?	
Who helped complete the task, and how?	

After Reading

After reading the story, ask:

❋ How does the Turkey Girl feel about herself in comparison to the other girls in the village? Why does she feel that way?

❋ Why do the turkeys want to help the girl get to the dance?

❋ What do the turkeys ask the girl to do in return for their kindness?

❋ Why doesn't the Turkey Girl arrive back at the cage in time?

❋ How does the Turkey Girl feel when she finds that the turkeys are gone? Why does she feel that way?

❋ *The Turkey Girl* is known as a how-and-why tale. It tells how something in nature came to be. What does this story explain?

Make a Mini-Book (Social Studies)

Make mini-books filled with facts about the Zuni Indians, using information children have learned from the story and facts from other resources, such as *The Zunis* (*True Books*) by Alice K. Flanagan (Children's Press, 1998). Include details such as where the tribe lived, what they did to survive (hunting, farming, fishing, and so on), and what kinds of homes they lived in. Position 8½- by 11-inch paper horizontally and cut across the center. Fold the paper in half, nest the pages, and staple along the left side to create mini-books.

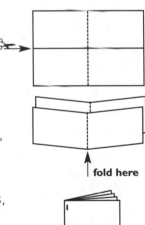

fold here

EXTEND IT!

Make a second mini-book that describes aspects of contemporary Zuni life.

Compare Clothing (Social Studies)

In *The Turkey Girl*, the turkeys created a dress of doeskin for their young care-taker. What kinds of clothing do the main characters wear in other Cinderella tales? Cut ten identical dresses from construction paper, approximately 8 by 10 inches. On each dress, write the title of a Cinderella tale you've read with the class. Then ask children to describe the clothing the main character wore to her special event, the fabric, if possible, and any jewelry, shoes, or other accessories worn. (In the case of Becan, describe his regular clothing,

including his bull's tail belt and special boots.) Write the description on the outfit. Stretch a length of string across a section of wall in the classroom. Use clothespins to hang the outfits in a row to make a clothesline display.

It's Festival Time! *Activity Page* (Social Studies)

The Turkey Girl wished to attend the Dance of the Sacred Bird, a Zuni festival. Use the reproducible on page 52 to compare the Dance of the Sacred Bird with other festivals. What might children find at a festival? Music? Dancing? Food? Dress? Special customs? Give each child two copies of the reproducible. Together, answer the questions about the Dance of the Sacred Bird on one turkey. Then ask children to think about a festival or celebration they've been to before and enjoyed. Have them think about it and answer the questions on the second turkey.

Story Frame (Language Arts)

Stories that explain events or circumstances in nature are called how-and-why tales, or *pourquoi* tales. Read aloud other examples of these types of stories, such as Rudyard Kipling's *Just So Stories* (William Morrow, 1996) or *Brother Wolf: A Seneca Tale* by Harriet P. Taylor (Farrar, Straus & Giroux, 1996). Invite children to explain how *The Turkey Girl* fits into this category of stories. Then brainstorm other topics for how-and-why tales, such as "why the cricket sings" and "how the squirrel got its long tail." Distribute copies of the reproducible on page 53. Have children work independently or in groups to choose their own how-and-why topics and write stories about them. Younger students might dictate their stories. For additional activities about teaching with *pourquoi* tales, visit **http://teacher.scholastic.com/ lessonrepro/lessonplans/pourquoitales.htm**.

Change the Ending (Language Arts)

Unlike most Cinderella stories, *The Turkey Girl* did not end happily ever after. The turkeys abandoned the girl when she failed to keep her word, and the girl felt sad to have let her friends down. Invite children to change or add to the ending of *The Turkey Girl* to make it either a happy ending or an ending in which the girl experiences growth and maturity. Perhaps she finds the turkeys and talks them into coming back. Perhaps she leaves the dance in time to get home before the turkeys go. Perhaps she is grateful that they left and goes on to find a new job in the community.

Tick, Tock, Story Clock (Language Arts)

Draw a circle on a sheet of white paper, and divide the circle into four equal parts. Number the parts one through four, and what have you got? A story clock! Have children make their own story clocks and use them as they retell the story of the Turkey Girl. In each section of the clock, children should write a sentence describing one part of the story, progressing from the beginning (section 1) to the end (section 4).

Imitate the Artist (Art)

Invite children to study illustrator Ed Young's pastel and oil crayon drawings in *The Turkey Girl*. Let children imitate the artist's style by sketching on dark construction paper with pastel chalk. Encourage children to blend chalk with their fingers to cover large areas and to imitate specific designs in Young's illustrations, such as the thin gates made of sticks and the round, white moon. Explain to students that they can draw abstract rather than realistic images, like those in *The Turkey Girl*.

Teacher-Tested Idea: Make an Origami Turkey (Art)

Teach your students to make fine-feathered friends of their own. Here's how:

1. Choose a sturdy piece of colored paper for the body, and cut it into a square.

2. Fold the paper in half along the diagonal, and then unfold.

3. As if you were making a paper airplane, fold the two corners into the center and then turn the paper over.

4. Fold the corners into the middle again.

5. Fold the top point to meet the bottom point.

6. Fold the smaller point down to make the head.

7. Fold up the end to make the tail.

8. Draw a face and add a paper wattle and paper or craft feathers.

Contributed by Linda Yoffe
Stamford, Connecticut

This activity appeared in *Fresh & Fun Thanksgiving* (Scholastic Professional Books, 1999).

It's Festival Time!

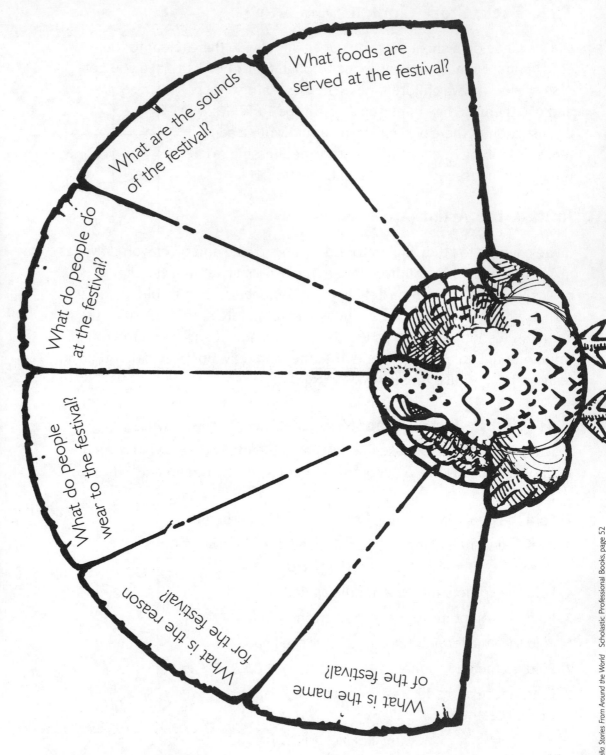

What foods are
served at the festival?

What are the sounds
of the festival?

What do people do
at the festival?

What do people
wear to the festival?

What is the reason
for the festival?

What is the name
of the festival?

Name _____

Date _____

Story Frame

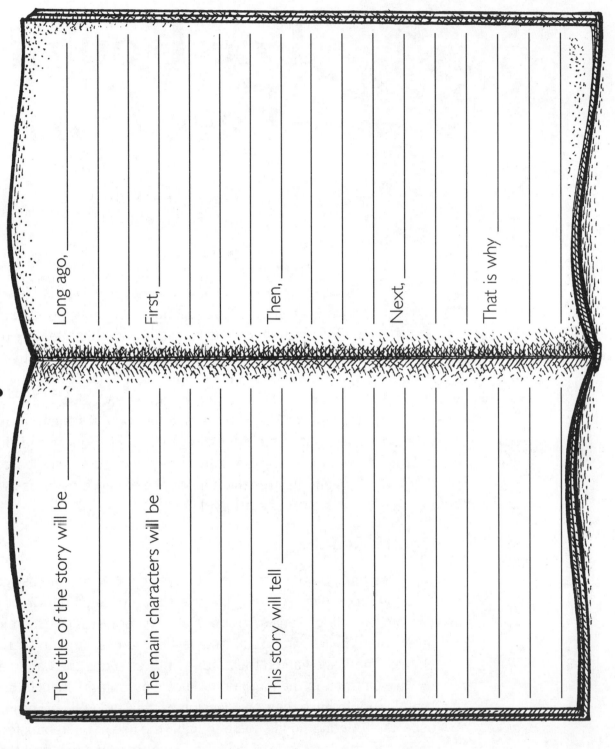

Long ago, _____

First, _____

Then, _____

Next, _____

That is why _____

The title of the story will be _____

The main characters will be _____

This story will tell _____

Teaching With Cinderella Stories From Around the World   Scholastic Professional Books

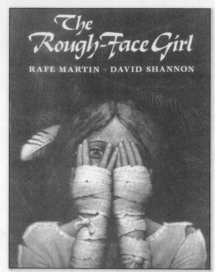

CANADA

The Rough-Face Girl

BY RAFE MARTIN
(G. P. Putnam's Sons, 1992)

Set on the shores of Lake Ontario, *The Rough-Face Girl* is an abbreviated version of the Algonquin Indian Cinderella. Similar to the Micmac legend The Invisible One, this tale tells the story of a young girl who is mistreated by her sisters and sets out to marry an invisible supernatural being. Algonquin legend has it that anyone who was able to see the Invisible Being would be rewarded by his hand in marriage. Clad in tree bark, the battered girl ignores the taunting of others and sets out to meet him. Because she is honest and kind, she is able to see what others cannot. Just like the culture it comes from, *The Rough-Face Girl* emphasizes the importance of nature, simple living, and respect for the power of earth and sky.

Before Reading

Display a large map of the United States and Canada, and ask children to find a group of five lakes. Explain that they are called the Great Lakes and are the world's largest group of freshwater lakes. Direct children's attention to Lake Ontario, the smallest of the five. Explain that a tribe of Native Americans named the Algonquin lived along the Canadian shores of Lake Ontario, in the region now known as Ontario. Tell children that the Algonquin have their own version of the Cinderella story. In it, many aspects of Algonquin life come to light: the use of birch bark for canoes and wigwams, the mode of cooking outdoors over a fire, and the need for camp-type living areas to allow for nomadic living. (Because they were hunters and gatherers, the Algonquin moved often, based on food supply.)

After Reading

After reading the story, ask:

❀ Why is the Rough-Face Girl treated cruelly by her sisters?

❀ What does the Rough-Face Girl do to prepare herself to see the Invisible Being?

❀ Why can't the sisters see the Invisible Being?

❀ How does the Invisible Being's sister prepare the Rough-Face Girl to see her brother?

❀ How does life change for the Rough-Face Girl once she can see the Invisible Being?

Make a Web of Algonquin Life (Social Studies)

Make webs to organize facts about Algonquin life long ago. Subjects for the web might include food, clothing, shelter, weapons, and travel. Students can glean much of this information simply by studying the words and illustrations in the story. Bring in reference books and other resources as needed. You might share *Little Firefly: An Algonquian Legend* by Terri Cohlene (Troll, 1991), another version of the Cinderella story that also includes cultural information.

Right the Wrongs (Social Studies)

Talk with children about the harsh treatment the Rough-Face Girl endured at the hands of her sisters. Invite them to think of ways to counter such treatment. Examples include being kind to those who have been unkind, seeking help from people who have the authority to stop the abuse, setting limits on the tasks one is willing to do, and expressing one's feelings through "I messages," such as "I feel angry when you speak harshly to me. I want you to talk to me with respect and kindness."

And the Winner Is . . . (Language Arts)

Invite children to name stories they've read or movies they've seen in which a gentle character is treated unkindly but goodness wins out in the end. Examples of such stories include *The Little Princess* by Frances Hodgson Burnett (Bantam, 1987; first published, 1905), *Farmer Duck* by Martin Waddell (Candlewick Press, 1991), and the classic folktales of Snow White, Hansel and Gretel, and The Ugly Duckling. List the characters on chart paper as children name them. Add to the list throughout the week as children recall other characters that fit the criteria.

Chart Comparisons (Language Arts)

Make a chart to compare and contrast Rafe Martin's *The Rough-Face Girl* with Perrault's *Cinderella*. In what ways are their homes, clothing, diet, chores, helper, and modes of travel the same or different?

Open Up! (Language Arts)

Explore characters in *The Rough-Face Girl* with easy-to-make story flaps. To make story flaps:

1. Fold a sheet of 8½- by 11-inch paper in half lengthwise.

2. Place the page horizontally on a flat surface.

3. Draw lines to divide the top half of the paper into thirds.

4. Cut along the lines, from the edge to the fold, to make three equal flaps.

5. On each flap, draw a picture of a different character from the story.

6. Lift each flap and write a description of the character underneath.

Personal Wigwams (Art)

The outside of the Invisible Being's great wigwam was painted with pictures of the sun, moon, stars, plants, trees, and animals. Ask children why they think the Invisible Being chose these items to adorn his home. Most likely, he chose items from nature because he loved nature and

because he was a part of it himself. Hand out 15-inch triangles of brown craft paper and ask children to pretend these are their wigwams. What will they draw on the outside that will tell others about themselves? Provide crayon or markers for drawing. Encourage children to think carefully before they draw and to choose each item for a specific reason rather than simply drawing for decoration. When finished, children can roll the paper into a cone with the artwork on the outside and tape it.

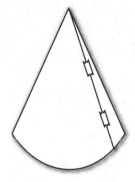

It's Only Natural (Art)

The Invisible Being held the rainbow and the Milky Way in his hands. Encourage children to make use of nature. Invite them to draw a picture that uses elements of nature as part of the image of a person or animal. For example, a giraffe might be represented as a tall oak tree that serves as its body and long, graceful neck. A person might use clouds for fluffy slippers, or a sliver of moon for a hammock. For inspiration, encourage children to close their eyes and imagine their visions of nature before they begin drawing.

EXTEND IT!

Bring in samples of nature from the great outdoors. Let children glue twigs, pussywillows, leaves, and shells to paper and then create animals or persons around them, intertwining the medium of art with nature.

How Constellations Came to Be (Science)

Challenge children to create stories about the origin of a constellation or group of stars. How did the Big Dipper get its name? Why are so many constellations named after characters from mythology? Have children tell their stories in a dark classroom.

EXTEND IT!

Invite children to create their own constellations. Have them draw their star patterns with glitter pens on dark blue paper (or they can use glue and rock salt or glitter). Encourage children to think of their shape before they begin to draw. Then have them invent a story of how their constellation came to be. Read aloud Greek myths for inspiration.

In the Night Sky **Activity Page** (Science)

Stars are hot balls of gas and dust that radiate heat and light and appear in the night sky as small points of light. Since ancient times, different people and cultures have grouped stars into recognizable patterns called constellations. Share four constellations with your students with this star-viewing craft. Here's what to do:

4–6

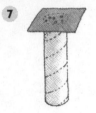

1. Hand out copies of the reproducible on page 59. Read and discuss the constellation cards.

2. Cover tables with layers of folded newspaper.

3. Choose a constellation from the pattern page and cut it out along the dotted line.

7

4. Give each student one sheet of black construction paper, cut into 3-inch squares. Place the black construction paper on top of the newspaper.

5. Place the constellation pattern that you selected on top of the black paper.

6. Use a pin to make a hole through each star in the constellation, piercing the black paper at the same time. Save the pattern to use again.

8–9

7. Center the black paper over one end of the tube so that the star pattern is within the opening.

8. Fold the paper around the tube and use a rubber band to hold it in place. Trim off excess paper.

10

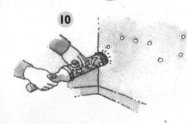

9. Tape the constellation card on the tube. Decorate your tube with neon paint (it glows in the dark!), star-shaped stickers, and glitter.

10. Hold the tubes toward a light and look through the open end to view the constellations. For a more dramatic effect, dim the lights and shine flashlights through the tubes, projecting the constellations onto a wall.

This activity appeared in *ScienceArt* by Deborah Schecter (Scholastic Professional Books, 1997).

Once Upon a Wigwam (Drama)

Divide the class into small groups. Ask each group to plan a short skit that tells the sequel to the story, explaining what happened after the Invisible Being married the Rough-Face Girl. What did the Rough-Face Girl call herself from then on? Where did they live? How did they interact with others? What elements of nature might the Rough-Face Girl have incorporated into her image, as the Invisible Being used the rainbow and Milky Way?

In the Night Sky

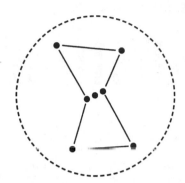

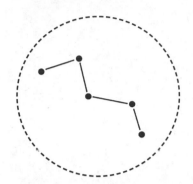

Orion

Orion was a famous hunter in Greek mythology. Three bright stars across his middle make his belt.

Cassiopeia

To the ancient Greeks, this group of stars looked like Cassiopeia, a powerful queen, sitting on her throne.

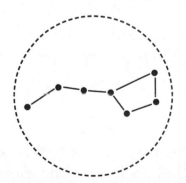

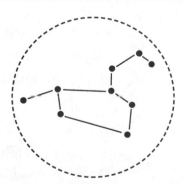

Big Dipper

These stars look like a giant ice cream scoop. The Big Dipper is part of a larger constellation called the Great Bear.

Leo

Leo means "lion." This star group looked like a lion to the ancient Greeks. Does it look like a lion to you?

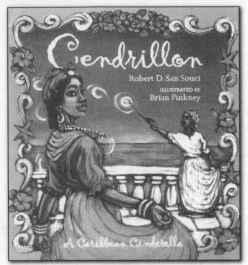

Cendrillon

BY ROBERT D. SAN SOUCI

(Simon & Schuster Books for Young Readers, 1998)

RELATED RESOURCES

Traditions From the Caribbean (Cultural Journeys) by Paul Dash (Raintree/Steck Vaughn, 1999) provides cultural information and colorful photographs that capture the flavor of the Caribbean.

The Caribbean (Food and Festivals Series) by Linda Illsley (Raintree/ Steck Vaughn, 1999) includes descriptions of celebrations and recipes.

Based on Charles Perrault's traditional *Cinderella*, *Cendrillon* has been written and illustrated to reflect West Indian culture, language, and costume. The story is set on the island of Martinique in the Caribbean and is told in the first person from the godmother's point of view, emphasizing the significance of the Creole oral tradition. The story follows the story line of Perrault's *Cinderella*, complete with godmother's magic, coach, gown, and slippers, but is set in the warmth of a tropical island and sprinkled with the native French Creole language.

Before Reading

Help children understand that an island is a body of land surrounded by water. Have them look on a world map or globe, and point out the island groups they see. Then direct their attention to a group of islands in Central America called the West Indies or Caribbean. Explain that the West Indies are made up of hundreds of islands. One of these is Martinique, one of the southernmost islands and the setting for *Cendrillon*. Martinique, called the Isle of Flowers, is home to lush green vegetation and tropical fruits such as bananas and pineapples. Discuss the fact that Martinique is governed by France and that many people who live there speak French.

After Reading

After reading the story, ask:

❋ How does Cendrillon become a servant in her own home?

❋ How does Cendrillon's godmother help her?

❋ Why doesn't Cendrillon want her godmother to help her see Paul a second time?

❋ Does Paul really care for Cendrillon? What part of the story tells you this?

A New Home for Cendrillon (Social Studies)

Invite students to study the illustrations in *Cendrillon*. What clues tell them about the physical environment in which the story takes place— its climate, landforms, plant life, scenery, and so on? In what ways do children think Cendrillon's life is affected by her physical environment? If her environment were different, would that change the kind of transportation she would use to get to the ball? The types of fruit available to serve as a coach? The clothing she wore or food she ate? Ask students to consider how Cendrillon's life (and the story) might be different if the tale took place in Alaska. Invite students to choose a different setting for the story, selecting something quite different from its present Caribbean setting. Have them write a simple summary of a new story or draw it in comic-strip form.

Make a Time Line (Social Studies)

Divide the class into groups and ask each group to make a time line tracking Cendrillon's life from birth to marriage. To make the time line, each group will need about eight sheets of construction paper in different colors. Each group member should be responsible for creating one or two segments of the time line, using a separate sheet of paper for each segment. Instruct students to begin at Cendrillon's birth, writing "Cendrillon born" or something similar and then illustrating the event. Then have them complete the time line in increments, writing and illustrating each landmark event in Cendrillon's life: her mother's death, her father's remarriage, her stepsister's birth and christening, and so on. Connect each group's segments with tape or staples, and display in the classroom.

Language Bingo (Language Arts)

Go through the story and ask children to point out French words, such as *agouti*, *manicou*, and *granmaison*. Read the sentences that include these words and invite children to guess their meanings. Write the words and their definitions on the board. (Verify the meanings and pronunciations by checking the glossary of French words at the back of *Cendrillon*.) Then use the words to play a game of Bingo. Here's how:

1. Leave the French words on the board, but erase the definitions.

2. On a sheet of white paper, draw a Bingo grid with five rows across and five down. Mark the center space FREE, and leave the other spaces blank. Photocopy the grid and give one to each child along with a handful of Bingo chips, plastic milk caps, or other markers.

3. Have children write the words from the list on their Bingo cards, placing one word in each space at random. If needed, words may be used twice to fill blank spaces.

4. Copy the words onto small index cards, and place them in a shoe box or paper bag.

5. To play the game, pick a card, read the word aloud, and invite volunteers to tell what it means in English.

6. As soon as someone correctly defines the word, the entire class may cover it on their Bingo cards. (Cover both words if the word is written twice.)

7. The first person to cover five spaces in a straight or diagonal line wins.

And Then What Happened? (Language Arts)

Cendrillon's story was told from her godmother's point of view. How would the tale have been different if the stepmother had told it? The father? Cendrillon herself? A spectator? Create a handmade microphone by taping a ball of aluminum foil to the top of a paper towel tube. Let children use the microphone to interview classmates posing as various characters in *Cendrillon*, getting the story from different points of view.

Fold a Story Activity Page (Language Arts)

Prepare children for this activity by discussing the main events that happened in *Cendrillon*. With children's help, write a sentence describing each of the events on the chalkboard. Distribute a copy of the reproducible

on page 65 and a square sheet of construction paper to each child. Help children follow the instructions to fold the storybook. Together, write on the four corners of the square, defining the story's characters, plot, setting, and conflict. Have children draw a picture in the center of the square, then fold in the flaps to close the story.

Thumbprint Strips (Language Arts)

Retell the story . . . thumbprint style! Provide washable inkpads and white paper. Let children press their thumbs in the ink and then on paper to make thumbprint cartoons. They can use the cartoons to explore the story; to compare and contrast point of view in *Cendrillon*, *Princess Furball*, and other stories; or to simply retell favorite scenes. The cartoons can be made up of one large scene or a strip of events. Post completed scenes for children to read and enjoy.

Teacher-Tested Idea: Ballroom Math (Math)

Make an interactive math bulletin board display. First, use craft paper (or contact paper with a design, unpeeled so it will not adhere) to create a basic ballroom scene on the bulletin board, including a simple wood dance floor and perhaps a backdrop that looks like wallpaper. Then draw and cut out simple shapes from sturdy paper that represent 10 women and 10 men, each approximately 4 inches tall. On the women, write a math problem based on Cinderella's ball, such as:

❀ If there were 70 women and 50 men at the ball, how many guests were there all together?

❀ If there were 45 men at the ball and twice as many women, how many women were there?

❀ If Cinderella arrived at the ball at 8:30 P.M. and stayed until midnight, how long was she at the ball?

❀ If the prince danced with 20 women per hour, how long did he dance with each one?

On the male figures, write the answers to the questions. Place the female figures in a large envelope stapled to the lower right corner of the bulletin board. Staple the male figures in random order onto the dance floor. Invite students to visit the bulletin board during free time, pick a woman from the envelope, and tape it beside the man who displays the correct answer to the question. Provide blank figures as well, and encourage students to make up their own ball-related word problems for classmates to solve.

Contributed by Sue Lorey
Arlington Heights, Illinois

Slipper Sleuth (Math)

Which kind of slipper do most Cinderellas wear—glass, gold, brocade? Or do they wear boots or sandals? Help children make a graph to find out. Create a four-column graph: Down the left column, write several kinds of slippers or shoes mentioned in Cinderella stories—for example, glass slipper, black boot, and golden sandal. Leave room for kids to draw a picture of each. Each time a shoe is featured in a Cinderella story, have children mark an X in the appropriate column of the graph. Let children add slippers as they read Cinderella stories that aren't featured in this book as well. When all tallies are in, have children count them to determine which is the most popular Cinderella-based footwear. Cap off the activity by hosting a slipper day in the classroom, on which students wear their own slippers to school.

	1	2	3
Loafer	X		
Golden Sandal	X		
Black Boot	X		
Glass Slipper	X	X	

Maracas Marathon (Art, Music)

Make Caribbean maracas using 6-ounce plastic spring water containers and beans. Give each child an empty, clean water bottle. Let children fill the bottle half-full with dried beans or popcorn kernels. Seal the lid tightly. Mix poster paints or acrylics with a bit of scouring powder so that the paint will adhere to the plastic bottles. Invite children to paint bright designs on their bottles, imitating the Creole patterns and coloring found in *Cendrillon*. When the designs are dry, spray with acrylic to seal. Let children shake them to their own Caribbean beat!

Fold a Story

Step 1

Fold construction paper in half to form two triangles, then open it.

Step 2

Fold two corners into the center.

Step 3

Fold remaining two corners to form a square.

Step 4

Write story information on the outside flaps of the square.

Step 5

In the center of the square, draw a picture to go with the story.

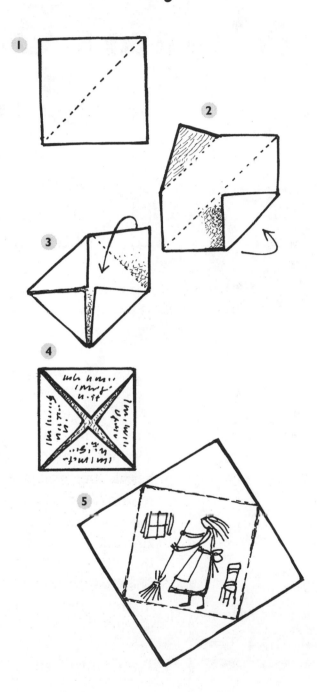

Mufaro's Beautiful Daughters:
An African Tale

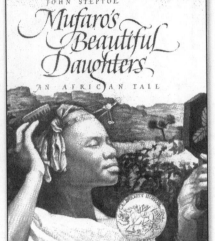

WRITTEN AND ILLUSTRATED BY JOHN STEPTOE

(Lothrop, Lee & Shepard Books, 1987)

Mufaro's Beautiful Daughters departs from traditional Cinderella tales in that there is no ball to attend, no dress to acquire, and no cruel guardian imposing harsh terms and conditions on a young girl's life. The story is similar to others, though, in that the main character finds joy in her life, treats all living things with kindness, and is eventually rewarded for her goodness. Set in an African rain forest, the story is filled with beauty and simplicity. Two sisters, one kind and one selfish, travel to a city for the chance to be wed to the king. Faced with the same opportunities along the way, only one shows compassion and generosity, and she is rewarded for it. African dress, communion with nature, and vibrant tropical wildlife bring authenticity to this African tale.

Before Reading

Mufaro's Beautiful Daughters is set in the ancient city of Zimbabwe. Familiarize students with the area before reading the story. Explain that Zimbabwe is a land of lush, tropical vegetation. People who live there might tend gardens, growing corn, sugar cane, and sweet potatoes, or they might raise sheep and other

animals. Animals such as elephants, antelopes, hippos, rhinoceroses, buffalo, and exotic birds live freely there. Help students locate Africa and then southern Africa on a world map or globe. Point to the location of Zimbabwe, and explain that the story takes place in that country.

After Reading

After reading the story, ask:

❀ What words would you use to describe Nyasha? Why would you describe her in this way?

❀ What words would you use to describe Manyara? Why would you describe her in this way?

❀ What tests do the sisters encounter along the way to the city? How do they respond?

❀ Why does the king choose Nyasha to be his wife?

❀ How do you think Manyara feels about herself and her behavior at the end of the story? Why do you think that?

Make Africa Shape Books (Social Studies)

The shape of the continent Africa lends itself well to a shape book. Trace the shape of Africa onto tagboard several times and cut out the shapes. Have children use the cutout shapes as a template with which to trace and cut out five identical shapes from craft or construction paper. Staple the pages together at the top, or have children punch holes and bind the pages with yarn to make a book. To find facts for the books, let children study *Mufaro's Beautiful Daughters* to learn about plant life, animal life, climate, and customs in southern Africa long ago. In addition, provide resources that offer a look at modern-day life in southern Africa. Have children record and illustrate interesting facts in their shape books.

A Moment in Time (Social Studies)

People make time capsules to preserve aspects of present-day life for future generations to see. Have children work alone or in small groups to make shoe box time capsules for Nyasha or the king. What would Nyasha or the king include that would tell others about their lives? Provide craft materials such as construction paper, glue, glitter, tissue paper, and pipe cleaners. Allow children to study the words and illustrations in *Mufaro's*

Beautiful Daughters to get ideas for their time capsules. As an example, Nyasha's time capsule might include a cutout of a water jug (symbolizing her work in the garden), a flower made of colorful tissue paper, a drawing of tall green crops (made beautiful by her songs), and a pipe cleaner snake (symbolizing her friend in the garden and, ultimately, her mate).

Weave a Web (Language Arts)

Make dual character webs to describe the personality traits of Nyasha and Manyara. At the center of each web, write the character's name and draw a circle around it. Draw six lines extending from the circle and draw an empty circle at the end of each line. In the circles, write six words that describe Nyasha. Do the same for Manyara.

Tree of Kindness *Activity Page* (Language Arts)

Compare how Manyara and Nyasha each treated the characters they encountered on their way to the city and what happened as a result. Distribute copies of the reproducible on page 70, and be sure children correctly identify Manyara and Nyasha. Starting at the top, have children read the question "How did she treat her sister?" and write an answer for each sister on its own leaf. Continue down the plant, answering all the questions. When children finish, discuss their answers and the importance of treating others—and all of nature—with kindness and respect.

African Animals *Activity Page* (Science)

The African continent is home to some of the most striking and colorful animals in the world. What kinds of animals live in southern Africa? Give each student a copy of the reproducible on page 71. Have children cut out the boxes and read the riddles. Then explain that they should draw the answer on the back of each, along with the name of the animal. (Answers: elephant, lion, giraffe, zebra) Children can make a mini-book of animal riddles by stacking the pages and stapling along the left side. Encourage students to research other African animals and write their own riddles to add to their mini-books.

How Many Snakes? (Math)

Nyasha's kindness to the snake proved to be central to the story's outcome. Use symbolic snakes to help students learn about measurement. Cut

various lengths of uncoated clothesline. Divide the class into pairs, and ask each pair to measure and record the length of their "snake." Then have each pair work together to measure ten objects in the classroom, defining the measurement of each by telling "how many snakes long" it is. Then have partners work together to calculate the true measurements by multiplying the length of each snake (in inches) by the number of snakes it took to measure the object.

Banners of Many Colors (Art)

Manyara and Nyasha wore clothing with beautiful designs. Let children create their own colorful fabric banners. You will need newspaper, fabric paint, kitchen sponges, several yards of plain muslin fabric, and 8-inch dowels.

1. Cut the fabric into 6- by 12-inch strips (one for each child).

2. Cut the sponges into thirds. Then cut these into shapes such as hearts, triangles, flowers, or snakes.

3. Cover a table with newspaper. Pour the paint into small saucers and place a selection of sponges beside each one. Give each child a fabric strip and invite a few children at a time to visit the paint station.

4. Let children dip sponges gently into the paint, rub off the excess on the sides of the saucer, and stamp the sponge onto the newspaper. When they are satisfied with their pattern, children can create it on their own fabric strips. Encourage children to work slowly and carefully, using different colors and sponges to create a deliberate pattern or design rather than simply stamping aimlessly.

5. After the fabric has dried, wrap one end tightly around the dowel and attach with duct tape, staples, or hot glue. (Caution: Be sure children understand that staple guns and hot glue guns are for adult use only.)

By the Beat of a Drum (Music)

Use a drum—even one as simple as an empty oatmeal container—to retell the story to music. Read the story aloud to drumbeats that move to a fast beat when the story grows exciting and a slow beat when the story seems calm.

Tree of Kindness

Manyara   **Nyasha**

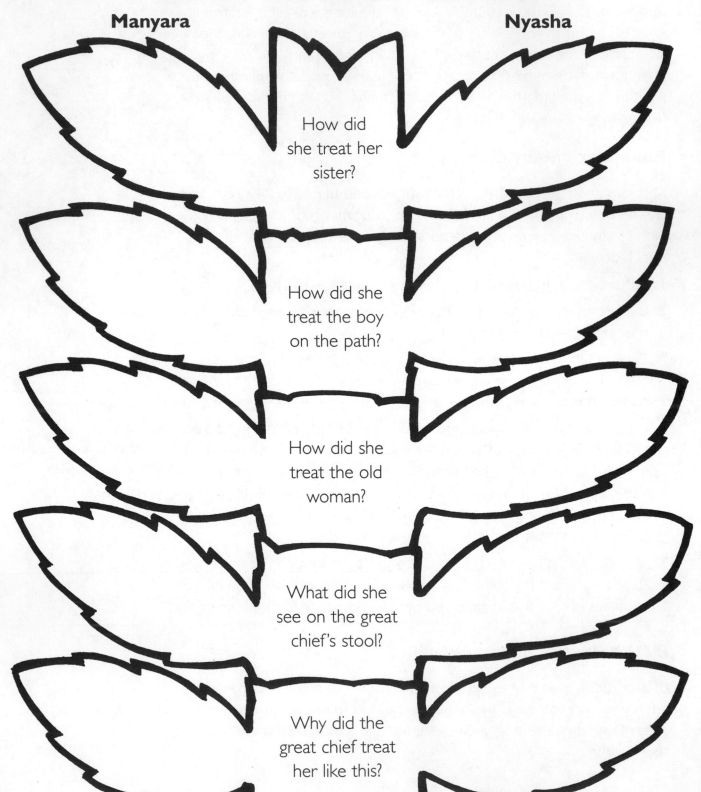

How did she treat her sister?

How did she treat the boy on the path?

How did she treat the old woman?

What did she see on the great chief's stool?

Why did the great chief treat her like this?

African Animals

Cut out the boxes below. Read each riddle.

On the back, write the name of the animal and draw a picture of it.

To make a mini-book, stack the boxes. Then staple along the left side.

My skin is loose and wrinkly.
My trunk is very long.
My ears are large,
I have two tusks,
and I am very strong.
What am I?

They say I am the king of beasts.
My roar will tell you that.
On grassy plains
I make my home.
I am a mighty cat.
What am I?

I am the tallest animal
of any you will see.
My legs and neck
are very long.
I eat leaves off the tree.
What am I?

I always travel with a herd
to keep me safe, of course.
My stripes are white
and brown or black.
I am a type of horse.
What am I?

Teaching With Cinderella Stories From Around the World Scholastic Professional Books

Cinder Edna

BY ELLEN JACKSON

(Lothrop, Lee & Shepard Books, 1994)

Based on the traditional tale of Cinderella—with an independent twist—*Cinder Edna* seeks to prove that fairy godmothers come from inside. The story tells of two girls living as neighbors, both of whom are forced to work for their wicked stepmothers and stepsisters. While one relies on magic to get to the ball, the other takes on a second job to pay for her dress and transportation.

Before Reading

Help students cross time periods as well as cultures to see how things have changed over the years. Bring in books, photographs, and anything you can find that shows pictures taken of women more than 30 years ago. Encourage children to study the pictures. Then ask students to tell how the lives of women have changed over the years. In what ways have they stayed the same? In what ways are they different? What opportunities (career, education, hobbies) are available to women today that were not available to women years ago? What can girls and women—as well as boys and men—do today to ensure that they will make use of the opportunities available to them?

After Reading

After reading the story, ask:

❈ In what ways are Cinderella and Cinder Edna alike and different?

❧ Who do you think is happier throughout the story: Cinder Edna or Cinderella? Why do you think that?

❧ What does it mean to be resourceful? What parts of the story show that Cinder Edna is resourceful?

❧ Why do Rupert and Cinder Edna have so much fun together?

❧ At the end of the book, the author wrote "Guess who lived happily ever after." What is your answer to that? Why do you feel that way?

I Can Do It! (Social Studies)

Cinder Edna relied on herself, not a fairy godmother, to get to the ball. She earned money to purchase a dress and a bus ticket. Talk with children about times when they need to rely on others (for example, for meals and shelter, when they are sick or hurt, or when they need to travel somewhere they cannot reach on foot or by bike) and times when they should try to rely on their own strengths and abilities (such as when they need to complete homework on time or when they need to solve a conflict with a friend). Invite children to draw a picture of themselves doing something that demonstrates independence—the ability to do something for oneself. Have them write a simple sentence to go along with the illustration.

Which Way to the Ball? (Social Studies)

Cinder Edna took a bus to the ball. How else might she have traveled there? Invite children to suggest other modes of transportation the modern heroine might have taken, such as a car, taxi, subway, bicycle, horse-drawn carriage, moped, or motorcycle. Have children draw pictures of these types of transportation and add them to a bulletin board display.

Cinder Edna's Big Book (Language Arts)

Write a collaborative class book modeled after Cinder Edna's examples of strength, independence, and ingenuity. Have children begin by creating their own character. Draw a stick figure on chart paper and invite children to develop the character as a group. Is the character a girl or boy? What is his or her age? Hair color? Height? What kinds of clothes does the character wear? Where does the character live—in a house, an apartment, a mobile home? How many people and pets in the family? Who are the

character's friends? What are his or her favorite foods, hobbies, and books? What are the character's strengths and weaknesses? Continue in this manner until the character's personality and background are well developed, as well as the setting in which the story takes place. Then let children work in small groups, creating stories about the character that demonstrate his or her strength, independence, and resourcefulness. Join these to make a collaborative book that tells not one story but many in the life of an admirable character.

Two Sides to Every Story? (Language Arts)

Sketch a generic figure on tagboard, similar in shape to the gingerbread man. Cut two identical copies of the figure for each child in your class. Have children glue or staple the figures together to make a two-sided person. Have them label one side of the person "Cinder Edna" and the other side "Cinderella." Have children decorate the characters and write sentences that tell about them, such as "Cinder Edna wears loafers," and "Cinderella wears glass slippers," or "Cinder Edna likes jokes and tuna casserole" and "Cinderella likes makeup and fancy clothes."

Make a Story Mural (Language Arts)

Together, determine eight main events in *Cinder Edna*. Write these on sentence strips, and place them in a pocket chart in random order. Work together to sequence the story's events. Then divide the class into eight groups. Assign each group one story event to re-create on a class story mural. Stretch a long strip of craft paper out across the classroom floor. Divide the strip into eight sections. Number the sections 1 to 8. Have each group work together to illustrate its portion of the time line and write a sentence describing what took place during that part of the story. Post the completed mural in the classroom or hallway. Invite children to retell the story to parents and other classroom visitors.

Make Change for the Bus *Activity Page* (Math)

Distribute copies of the reproducible on page 76 and have students calculate the money Cinder Edna might earn and what it would enable her to buy. You might want to give students play money to help them find the answers. This activity can be done independently or in groups.

Rupert's Recycling (Science)

Rupert and Edna cared about the world around them. As a result, they both recycled. Ask students to find examples in *Cinder Edna* that demonstrate recycling and other ways of caring for the environment: taking a bus to conserve fuel, recycling plastic at the ball, installing solar heating on Cinder Edna and Rupert's home, studying waste disposal engineering, and caring for orphaned kittens. Talk with students about these and other ways to care for the environment. Review materials that can be recycled and reused: paper, cardboard, plastic, aluminum, glass, and so on, and ask students to list other means of demonstrating environmental responsibility, such as picking up trash, putting litter in its place, conserving water, carpooling to conserve fuel, planting trees and flowers, and conserving electricity. Have students work in small groups to write and illustrate an addition to the story that involves one or more of these elements.

Sun Power (Science)

Rupert and Edna used solar power to heat their home. On a sunny day, use this activity to give students a firsthand look at the heating power of the sun.

1. Divide the class into four groups. Give each group two identical trays containing one of each item: 2-inch square of milk chocolate, custard cup filled with cool water, custard cup holding one ice cube, and a thermometer.

2. Take students outside. Find a place in direct sunlight. Have each group leave one sample tray in the sun.

3. Find a very shady spot. Have each group leave its second sample tray in the shade.

4. Have students record important data at the beginning of the experiment, such as the appearance (or temperature, if applicable) of each sample. Then invite them to predict what they think might happen if they leave the sample there for 30 minutes and for two hours.

5. After 30 minutes, have students observe and then test the temperature or solidity of each sample. Have them write their observations in their notebooks.

6. After two hours, have students observe and record their findings, compare them to their predictions, and write conclusions. What did they learn about solar power?

Make Change for the Bus

Cinder Edna earns $1.50 an hour for cleaning birdcages and mowing lawns.
Use this information to answer the questions below.

1. Cinder Edna wants to buy food for her kittens. A 10-pound bag of food costs
$9. How many hours will Cinder Edna need to work to earn the money?

_____

2. Cinder Edna wants to take Rupert to a recycling fair. Tickets to the fair cost
$12.50 each. How many hours will Cinder Edna need to work to earn
enough money for the tickets? _____

3. Cinder Edna worked 20 hours last week. Now she has enough money to buy
some of the things she's been wanting. How much money did she earn last
week? _____

Now look at the price list below. Which items is Cinder Edna able to buy?
Circle the items, making sure that the total cost is less than or equal to the
amount of money Cinder Edna earned last week.

Joke book $3

Music book for the accordion $12

Flower seeds $2

Cookbook $15

Watering can $4

24 cans of tuna fish $20

4. Cinder Edna wants to save money. She plans to put half of what she earns in
the bank. How many hours will Cinder Edna need to work in order to put
$30 in the bank? _____

Teaching With Cinderella Stories From Around the World   Scholastic Professional Books

Cinderella: A Celebration

Wrap up your study of Cinderella with a day of fun and festivity!
(**Note:** Some of the activities below require advance planning.)

 Teacher-Tested Idea:

Cultural Cuisine (Social Studies)

What type of cuisine might have been served at Cinderella's ball? Invite children to browse through cultural and ethnic cookbooks to find simple recipes from various cultures. Divide the class into small groups and assign each group one of the Cinderella stories. Have children work together to prepare a menu for the ball that reflects the culture from which their version of Cinderella originated. Have each group share its completed menu with the class. If possible, invite volunteers to bring in sample finger foods or desserts from their menus. What a wonderful way to add a tasty twist to the study of Cinderella!

Contributed by Sue Lorey
Arlington Heights, Illinois

Cinderella Went to the Ball . . .
(Language Arts)

Play a quick alphabet memory game. Gather the class in a circle. Start the game by saying "Cinderella went to the ball. On her way she dropped an apple." Go around the circle, with each successive player adding an item to the story that begins with the next letter of the alphabet. For example, the second player might say, "Cinderella went to the ball. On her way she dropped an apple and a ball . . ."

Which Cinderella Is Which?
Activity Page (Language Arts)

Hand out the reproducibles on pages 78–79. Have children work independently to read each riddle and write the appropriate character's name and story title.

The Votes Are In (Math)

Graph students' favorite Cinderella stories. Assign 10 volunteers the task of drawing pictures to represent each of the Cinderella stories you've studied together. Post the pictures on the wall around the classroom. Invite children to stand under the picture describing the story they like best. Tally the votes to determine which Cinderella story is the most popular.

Dressmaker, Dressmaker, Make Me a Dress (Art)

Provide drawing paper and crayons. Ask children to design a new dress or carriage for any of the Cinderellas. Challenge students to think of other objects besides a pumpkin that could have been used as a carriage or other outfits Cinderella might have worn instead of a dress.

Character Dialogue (Drama)

What if characters from different stories met each other? What advice would they give each other? What questions would they ask? Have students work in pairs to choose two characters from different stories. Challenge children to think of a brief dialogue the characters might have and perform it for the class.

Which Cinderella Is Which?

1 Smoke and ashes scarred her skin,
but nothing hurt her sight.
When she saw the rainbow,
things started to go right.
Character's Name: _____
Title of Story: _____

2 Walnut shells are very small,
but this princess was wise.
What she put into the shells
was part of her disguise.
Character's Name: _____
Title of Story: _____

3 Animals came to her rescue
when the job seemed much too great.
Though her family tried to stop her,
one small slipper changed her fate.
Character's Name: _____
Title of Story: _____

4 In the darkness of the night,
dressed in beauty, she did dance.
When she failed to keep her promise,
she received no second chance.
Character's Name: _____
Title of Story: _____

5 She cleaned cages for the money
that it cost to buy a dress.
Wise and clever and hardworking,
she could make her own success.
Character's Name: _____
Title of Story: _____

Teaching With Cinderella Stories From Around the World Scholastic Professional Books

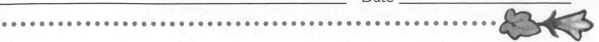

6 Out of love, her real godmother
waved a magic wand about.
Mice and lizards, rats and pumpkins
changed their form to help her out.
Character's Name: _____
Title of Story: _____

7 She was kind to all who knew her.
Snakes and people were her friends.
With her song, she tended flowers.
Goodness won out in the end.
Character's Name: _____
Title of Story: _____

8 With a belt, he scared an ogre
and sank a dragon like a barge.
With his boots he won a princess.
His two feet were mighty large!
Character's Name: _____
Title of Story: _____

9 Magic fish bones served her kindly.
For the goodness she had shown.
Life changed when a tiny slipper
fit her foot and hers alone.
Character's Name: _____
Title of Story: _____

10 When the clock was striking midnight,
she was running down the stairs.
One glass slipper, left behind her,
soon would take away her cares.
Character's Name: _____
Title of Story: _____

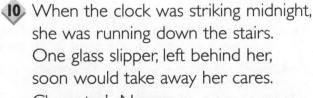

Additional Resources

Books for Teachers

Children Just Like Me by Barnabas and Anabel Kindersley (Dorling Kindersley, Ltd., 1995) takes an in-depth look at the lives of children around the world. One child is featured for each country included in the book. Through photographs, quoted interviews, and narrative text, readers get a firsthand look at the child's family, home, school, favorite foods and toys, and more.

Children's Traditional Games: Games From 137 Countries and Cultures by Judy Sierra and Robert Kaminski. (Oryx Press, 1995). A treasury of children's games from around the globe.

Cinderella by Judy Sierra (Oryx Press, 1992). A comprehensive collection of Cinderella stories from around the world, each prefaced with information on the story's origin. Includes detailed footnotes, glossary, activity ideas, and recommended reading lists.

Eight Cinderellas by Nancy Polette (Pieces of Learning, 1997) highlights eight Cinderella tales and provides lists of projects and activities to accompany each one.

A Fresh Look at Fairy Tales by Theda Detlor (Scholastic, 1995). This thematic unit takes an in-depth look at gender bias in Cinderella and other well-known fairy tales, offering a teacher-tested plan for combating bias and increasing student awareness.

Multicultural Fables and Fairy Tales by Tara McCarthy (Scholastic, 1992) presents activities to broaden literary and cultural awareness through a study of trickster tales, fables, why stories, and fairy tales.

Web Sites

The Children's Literature Web Guide
http://www.ucalgary.ca/~dkbrown/cinderella.html
This site lists variations on the Cinderella story and specific teaching ideas.

The Doucette Index: Teaching Ideas for Children's Books
http://www.educ.ucalgary.ca/litindex
This site features a comprehensive index of books and Web sites that support literature-based instruction.

Shen's Books
http://www.shens.com
A listing and review of Cinderella stories around the world.

The Web English Teacher
http://www.webenglishteacher.com/myth.html
A resource of activities, lesson plans, and electronic text of Cinderella stories around the world.

Books for Children

Angkat: The Cambodian Cinderella by Jewell Reinhart Coburn (Shen's Books, 1998). A young girl befriends a fish and receives the gift of golden slippers, which eventually lead her to the heart of a prince.

Cinder-Elly by Frances Minters (Viking, 1994). Told in rap, this urban tale tells of a young girl ridiculed by her sisters and befriended by a fairy godmother who helps her find the boy of her dreams at a basketball game.

The Golden Sandal: A Middle Eastern Cinderella Story by Rebecca Hickox (Holiday House, 1998). A young girl finds love with the help of a fish and a dainty gold sandal. Based on a Cinderella story from Iraq.

The Golden Slipper: A Vietnamese Legend by Darrell Lum (Troll Associates, 1994) is a traditional tale of a kindhearted girl who is mistreated by her stepfamily.

Jouanah: A Hmong Cinderella by Jewell Reinhart Coburn and Tzexa Cherta Lee (Shen's Books, 1996). Despite her cruel stepfamily, a young Hmong girl finds happiness with the help of her dead mother's spirit and a pair of dainty shoes.

Moss Gown by William H. Hooks (Clarion Books, 1987). Misunderstood by her father, Candace is sent away from her childhood home in the South. Years later, in a moss gown transformed, she captures the heart of a young man and also reunites with her father.

Nomi and the Magic Fish by Phumla (Doubleday & Company, 1972). Set in the heart of Africa, this Zulu tale features a young girl named Nomi, a wicked stepfamily, and a magic fish.

The Persian Cinderella by Shirley Climo (HarperCollins, 1999). A girl gives money to the poor rather than using it to buy herself a dress for a New Year celebration.

Prince Cinders by Babette Cole (Putnam, 1997). Set in the 1990s and filled with humorous twists and fun illustrations, this delightful spoof presents the male perspective on the traditional Cinderella. Brothers take the place of stepsisters, and the overworked Prince Cinders rides to a disco party instead of a ball.

Raisel's Riddle by Erica Silverman (Farrar, Straus, and Giroux, 1999). A poor orphan works in the kitchen of a Rabbi's home until her wisdom and kindness are discovered and rewarded.

Smoky Mountain Rose by Alan Schroeder (Dial Books for Young Readers, 1997). High in the Smoky Mountains, a girl named Rose sees her wishes come true with the help of a magical hog.